SANYAAS IN THE CITY

SANYAAS IN THE CITY

The Urban Dweller's Guide to Inner Freedom

ADARSH GUPTA
NEHA SAREEN | SHIKHA MEHRA
with DR MICKEY MEHTA

HAY HOUSE INDIA
New Delhi • London • Sydney
Carlsbad, California • New York City

Hay House Publishers (India) Pvt Ltd
Muskaan Complex, Plot No. 3, B-2, Vasant Kunj, New Delhi – 110070, India

Hay House LLC, P.O. Box 5100, Carlsbad, CA 92018-5100, USA
Hay House UK Ltd, 1st Floor, Crawford Corner, 91-93 Baker Street, London W1U 6QQ, UK
Hay House Australia Publishing Pty Ltd, 18/36 Ralph St., Alexandria NSW 2015, Australia

Email: contact@hayhouse.co.in
Website: www.hayhouse.co.in

The images have been provided by author Neha Sareen.

First published by Hay House India, 2024
Reprint, 2024
11 10 9 8 7 6 5 4 3 2

ISBN 978-93-6611-679-2
ISBN 978-93-6611-384-5 (E-Book)

Printed at Replika Press Pvt Ltd

FSC
www.fsc.org
MIX
Paper | Supporting responsible forestry
FSC™ C016779

Hay House is committed to a sustainable future for our business, our readers and our planet. This book is made from Forest Stewardship Council® certified paper.

This book is dedicated to the invisible guiding force that inspired us to take the Sanyaas mindset to the millions of city dwellers worldwide living a life not aligned with their intrinsic nature. We experienced three incredible years of intuitive thinking and writing, with the singular purpose of pouring from our hearts to make a quantum difference in people's lives. We are eternally thankful to the light of unity consciousness for choosing us to be the messengers of the new path-breaking Soul Mind way of thinking . . .

Authors Neha Sareen (left), Adarsh Gupta (centre top), Shikha Mehra (right), and Dr Mickey Mehta (centre bottom)

Contents

Preface

Nature

'To know what that true self is without social pressure is to know your true nature.'
—Martha Beck

Nature is how God made everything. There is a divine design to everything! The word 'nature' draws us towards its enormity, beauty, utility, and interconnectedness. We marvel at the thought of being in nature. There must be a reason for us to feel uplifted and peaceful in nature-rich conditions. For most of us, the real reason eludes our comprehension. All we know is that it draws us back to calm our frazzled nerves.

We have witnessed, with awe and wonder, how nature has shaped the lives of millions of species over the ages. Millions of years ago, life was restricted to unicellular existence. Gradually, these cells formed communities and, finally, grouped themselves intelligently into thinking forms, living in harmony. This harmony largely existed until we humans, the most intelligent part of nature's equation, got caught up in a mad chase for material gain. The fallout of this chase has taken its toll on a substantial part of the world's population over time, alongside the gradual degradation of nature's womb around our planet.

The mystery of nature stems from its seamless interconnectedness. For example, when we observe nature at play in a jungle, we cannot help but be astounded by the synchronistic intermingling and thriving of a vast ecosystem, which includes animals, birds, trees, algae, water bodies, and the role of climate on them all. While most of us are aware of and can relate to nature operating in automatic mode, our ego mind makes us believe that we are a towering superimposition on everything around us. This is the main reason why most of us disregard nature. We like to feel and enjoy its beauty with absolute insensitivity towards protecting or harnessing it.

In our entire construct of existence, particularly in urban settings, there is a colossal slip in our characterisation of nature. We tend to overlook that we humans are the most sophisticated life form of nature on Earth. We become victims of the narrative that nature is everything outside of us. There is, however, an inner world of nature. Our inner world consists of billions of cells intelligently formed into the various parts of our bodies and nurtured by streams of blood and water. Beyond the physical or visible body, multiple bodies comprise our existence. These bodies include our mental body, vital body, and most importantly, supramental body, which is also referred to as our soul in the realm of spirit. Much like the jungle example, our inner world has a lot of nature happening inside.

The moment we wake up to the scientifically and logically discerned inner-to-outer nature equation, we begin to see our inner and the varied forms of nature in the world around us as seamlessly interconnected. Our physical structure is ever-changing, yet we believe our physicality is the true self. However, the observer of this changing body form is our true identity. This observing true self is our real nature at play with our physical form and everything that surrounds it. This realisation is the start of sowing the seed of a yearning to understand our true origins.

The findings of quantum physics corroborate this seamless interconnectedness. According to this science, everything in our universe, including all living and non-living things, operates from a field of unity consciousness. This is a field outside the space-time world we live in and relate to. It is a field of pure potentiality. Quantum physics suggests that everything exists as a wave of possibility in unity consciousness until we transform the chosen possibility into an actuality. For evolved souls, this collapse happens through a state of flow that allows the voice of intuition to guide them with absolute clarity and connectedness. For materialists, the ego gets in the way of pure intuition, creating non-aligned paths that invariably lead to dissatisfaction or accidents over time.

The ultimate scientists who have strived to unravel the truth of human nature and its natural connection to the world of unity consciousness are the eternal yogis. These fascinating beings have spent lifetimes in solitude, dedicating hours, days, and years to deep meditation—an endeavour most of us would consider madness. A life full of deep meditative practice, without the need for food, water, or sex for days on end, does not come naturally to most of us. The quest of these yogis has been to unravel the mystery of existence through countless births. In this time spent in supposed madness, they have decoded the human genome beyond genetics, epigenetics, and other frontiers of recorded science.

The world of science and logic has been researching the mystic claims of spiritualists. The answers, as they come to light, increasingly reinforce the claims made by the yogis. Knowledge-based forums are mushrooming across the world, bringing together the best minds from both worlds to bridge the gap.

The 8.1 billion people in the world today are 8.1 billion unique creations of nature.

This book is a humble endeavour to shine a light on the true nature of us humans. We aim to shift your perspective from relating nature solely with the external world to diving deep within, to witness the beauty, enormity, and uniqueness of each of us. We are from nature and are nature ourselves. The entire equation changes the moment we realise the truth about being nature. A human fully in tune with their core engages in a seamless interplay between the inner and outer worlds. In this way of thinking, the perception of the body dissolves, leaving nature at play with nature. There are no boundaries in this understanding of life. There is just bliss, selfless love, and a burning desire to listen to our instinct to give from our internal to the external world.

It is time for us to live our very own nature-inspired love story.

Introduction

The Building Blocks of Sanyaas

'"I do not want to get material life, do not want the sense-life, but something higher." That is renunciation. Then, by the power of meditation, undo the mischief that has been done.'

—Swami Vivekananda

Haven't we all imagined a fairy-tale world where everything is picture-perfect? A world full of happiness, love, and laughter—a place where we do what we desire and thrive. In this world, curiosity makes us experience every moment with a sense of wonder. It is a magical place where everything you imagine is achievable with a true heart. Here, people believe in the inherent goodness of humans and bring out the brightest and best versions of each other. There is purity, innocence, and play. We are fully in tune with our inner selves to make the most of the outer world. We are guided by our truest friend, intuition, which, in turn, is led by the invisible higher power.

Sanyaas is home to living a life of truth, consciousness, and bliss. On this path of living, we are true to our inner self and not misguided by the conditioning and pressure of the external world. We are conscious and living from the point of an observer of life, connected yet not enslaved by the physical confines of our bodies. This is an experience of bliss in every moment of everything. We are not torn about the past or worried about the future but are wholly invested in the present moment for what it is. Such is the body and structure of living the life of a sanyaasi.

The essence of a sanyaasi lies in the understanding of the truth about the immortality of the soul. It involves transcending the biggest fear of our lives—death. It is about knowing we will remain in the soul form even after our death. It is about knowing that the soul will reincarnate in a new body or a new life and that the soul's journey will continue until all our karmas from all births are resolved.

In this knowing, we experience true fearlessness. We start to observe life in the physical form from a distance and become unshakable at the level of the soul. We begin to experience life without boundaries or excessive susceptibility to any situation. We start to think and act from the mind of our Soul, the Soul Mind, as opposed to the mind of our body, the Body Mind.

Our soul loves bliss. The Soul Mind pushes us towards our true nature, influencing every dimension of our life, impacting our gravitation towards what we do, who we spend time with, what we eat, how we think, and even how we have sex. We start to experience the beauty of living every moment in bliss, and this becomes our default setting.

We can trace the origins of Sanyaashood to ancient India, where rishis and spiritual masters sought answers to life's biggest questions. This deep search within included seeking the truth to questions like 'Who am I?' 'What is my purpose?' 'Is there a God?' 'Is there life after death?' 'Is there a connection between our life and God?' They were revered as awakened masters or gurus, having realised the distilled truth of life and beyond. Over time, Sanyaas evolved into a science with a set of logical steps leading to the stairway of enlightenment. This is called the science of yoga.

Most of us are conditioned to think of Sanyaas as a tough way of life. We are wired to think of Sanyaas as a path of renunciation, seclusion, and a very torturous life choice with no material gain at the end of this sacrifice. This perspective has been shaped by how Sanyaas has been represented throughout history. However, the essence of this way of life is anything but that.

The reality that we will elaborate on throughout this book is that we can lead the life of a monk even in an urban environment. It requires a profound shift in perspective and values, leading to a life of simplicity, connectedness, service, and meaning, with potential material gains.

Sanyaas in the context of city life is not about physically escaping our current reality or leaving behind our relationships and responsibilities. It takes more courage to live in our reality and rise above it. Sanyaas is about transcending the boundaries of the mind while going through life. When ego, duality, and delusions have no power over us and we can go beyond the limitations of the mind, we transcend the mind of our body. One of the greatest spiritual luminaries of our time, Osho, beautifully described Sanyaas as the culmination of our understanding of worldly conflicts.

The ancient Indian life guide, The Bhagavad Gita, throws light on the *gunas* or qualities of a true sanyaasi that can help us transcend the material landscape of our existence. As you absorb the six gunas of a sanyaasi, you may find yourself releasing previous biases towards your current comprehension of Sanyaas, making space for a new understanding.

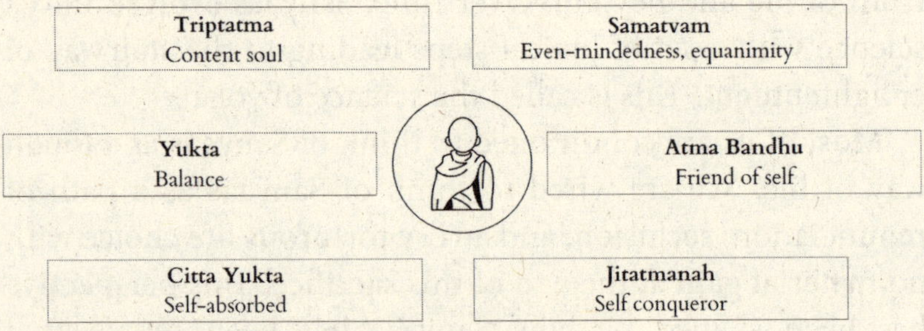

Six Gunas of a Sanyaasi

Samatvam—Even-Mindedness

This is the guna of even-mindedness and equanimity that helps a person not react or get disturbed by the changing circumstances—positive or negative—of life. Have you ever observed a see-saw in a park? It moves up and down but the pivot, which is its central part, remains fixed—unmoved and unaffected. Can we train our minds to be the stable pivot in the see-saw of our life? Yes, we can do so by operating from the Soul Mind as opposed to the Body Mind. This virtue requires effort to uncover your true self from the dust of societal conditioning. According to the Bhagavad Gita, an individual who develops this guna is liberated from all external attachments and expectations.

Atma Bandhu—Friend of Self

In Sanskrit, atma means 'soul' and bandhu means 'true friend'. A true sanyaasi needs the atma to be the ultimate go-to friend of the self. We are conditioned to look outwards in the direction of family, friends, and mentors for support, advice, reassurance, and validation. In reality, we are all on singular journeys that are well and truly experienced at a singular level. This phenomenon is best explained by the individual suffering that one goes through in times of disease.

Can you imagine being your own best friend where you receive boundless love, support, encouragement, honesty, and, above all, the right direction from within? Think about how your experience of life would evolve if you had such a connection with your true self.

Jitatmanah—Self Conqueror

If our Body Mind is the dominating force in our journey, how can we then transcend this mind state towards higher possibilities? We all experience the power battle between the mind of our body and the soul from time to time. Life would be blissful in situations where the Soul Mind is our true guide and dominates the callings of the Body Mind. The virtue of listening to and following the wisdom of the soul versus the whispers of the mind elevates an individual's ability to evolve beyond the scope of the mind itself. The path to self-realisation can only occur when we have truly conquered the mind. For this, we need to rise above the dualities of life—such as success and failure, pleasure and pain based on the erstwhile Newtonian world view of cause and effect—and rejoice in the victories of the soul in the battles with the mind. Jitatmanah leads to the ultimate victory for the human being—victory over the monkey mind. Simply put, it is the ultimate state of mind control.

Triptatma—Content Soul

When our mind is racing faster or slower than its natural flow, we are in a state of imbalance. The mind is shaken or stirred; our soul is at peace. The mind is chasing; our soul is unhurried. We cannot demand a bud to bloom into a flower faster than its natural pace, just as we cannot control the speed at which the Earth rotates around the Sun. Nature unravels at its own pace and time.

It is important to note that our natural pace can vary at different stages of our lives. In our younger years, the natural pace will be a lot faster as compared to our older years. The idea here is to observe the natural pace from the Soul Mind and align it with the Body Mind. Our mind's attachment to events in the past or expectations of the future keeps it over- or under-paced. While it is important to have a vision to work towards, it is equally important not to be consumed by the desire for immediate results or any results at all.

A sanyaasi cultivates the ability to go with the natural flow without worrying about outcomes. The key here is to focus on doing what comes naturally in every moment without any expectations. Such a person can truly accept everything in life, including both the positives and negatives, as supreme grace, and acknowledge the countless blessings in their life.

Yukta—Balance

Too much or too little of anything is not good. A life lived in extremes attracts *dukha* or sorrow. A life lived in balance is a life lived with joy. Most people swing in the extremes of either self-indulgence or self-denial, forgetting that the law of cause and consequence shadows us wherever we go. Practicing the art of living a balanced life not only prevents the fallout from extreme actions but also trains you to make conscious choices in living a life of self-attention and love. An individual with the guna of yukta is known to do and be in balance with everything in life. They adopt a moderate approach to eating, drinking, sleeping, thinking, and expressing emotions. These individuals find balance and harmony in all aspects of life.

Citta Yukta—Self Absorbed

This guna withdraws the Citta or mind from the external material world, desires, cravings, and sensory pleasures, moving you inwards, connecting with your true nature and the higher power.

The three pillars of *seva* (selfless service), *sadhana* (practice), and *dhyana* (meditation) help us unfold this experiential truth. With *seva*, we understand the simplicity of us coming from nature and the need for us to give back. *Sadhana* keeps us yearning constantly to seek the deeper truths of our soul world. And *dhyana*, as guided by gurus or spiritual masters, is the science of getting there. With thorough discipline, yoga practices, and an unwavering faith in the Supreme intelligence, an individual can attain the state of Citta Yukta.

You must have some clarity now as to where you stand on the Sanyaas state of mind. Whatever your current reality, you can experience the higher truths of a sanyaasi by first creating an intent to get there.

This Sanyaas state of mind comes with a promise of hopefully putting you back on your inner track to help you realise the wonders of the world you once imagined as being life. Some of us may be seeking this transformation as individuals, but can you imagine the impact of a collective movement embracing the Sanyaas way of life? The world would be a blissful place to live in, and nature would bless us in miraculous ways.

The mention of Sanyaas stirs a sense of intrigue to understand this unique profession. It draws hordes of people each year and has done so through the years of documented history. This profession has no promise of name, fame, material gain, or comfort, yet it magnetises people to hop on this journey. How can these people achieve a sense of contentment this deep without a hefty salary or a big mansion or a glitzy car? How can a chase for nothing lead to a life of love, peace, tranquillity, and wisdom? These are the kinds of questions that do cross our minds. For many, it leads us to explore this unique profession in our little ways.

People on a material quest often narrate stories of how they had never bothered to look inwards. Inside is where your truth resides. This inner quest is deliciously addictive. Its high is a better and more sustained high compared to the transient intoxication of drugs, alcohol, fame, money, or material achievements. This is a high generated in our mind and bears no side effects. It allows you to go beyond the mind where you are not limited by the boundaries of thought itself. This is the quantum field of manifestation, where we go beyond the known into the unknown realms of creativity.

The encouraging part is that this natural mind state can be attained wherever you are, doing whatever you might be doing, and with minimal disruption to your existing pattern. This life-transforming track of Sanyaashood can be pursued concurrently with your current life.

This book has been written for you to gain clarity about this paradigm of this parallel way of living. This parallel track should have been your default track if you were not distracted by the conditioning of the world. You will be the best judge to evaluate how much of which track to accelerate on, depending on how you feel the two tracks evolve. This quest to integrate the core values of a sanyaasi is critical if you are committed to making the most of this life and beyond.

Sanyaas in the City has been written with a clear intent of demystifying this complex and abstract world for most people to understand. It will lay bare the fundamentals of the Sanyaas way of life and help you get on the path. For the millions of people who yearn to get on this path or have taken the first step through the practice of yoga asanas, this will be a door opener to the next logical steps on the path of yoga, which is the complete union of the Body Mind with the Soul Mind.

For the uninitiated, this book will be a great guide to understanding the virtues of getting on this path. This is intended to be a comprehensive framework that addresses the body, mind, and spirit. As we get started, we will experience the absolute interconnectedness firsthand.

Just jump in, there is something for everyone.

1
The Invisible Web

'Let your soul stand cool and composed before a million universes.'

—Walt Whitman

Most of the popular content streaming platforms like Netflix and Amazon Prime have created a multi-billion-dollar formula for success—hook the viewer's attention within the first five to ten minutes with a shocking event, and you have got the audience living the show! Isn't this also happening to most of us in real life? Human nature is such that it takes a jolt to pause, reflect, and realign with our intrinsic selves.

Confusion, suffering, fatigue, boredom, health complications, trauma, or even the death of a loved one or the end of a relationship can trigger the journey of an inner awakening, encouraging us to question our choices and life paths. These physical, mental, and emotional disturbances affect all of us. You are not alone.

In the normal course of chasing material heights, we tend to get so consumed that we forget to prioritise ourselves before anything we might potentially gain. This phase is packed with pace, excitement, social manoeuvring, and an undying need to grow and succeed at any cost—even at the cost of harming ourselves. This chase, full of stresses and strains, leads us to seek synthetic anchorage in need-based relationships and habits like smoking, excessive drinking, binge, or inadequate eating, or even indulgences like multiple sexual partners, to name a few. Interestingly, while going through these phases, we completely believe in this way of life as the best path. This fast-paced and chaotic way of living has become the norm.

Most of us tend to have this fire within to grow. As it is said, you are either growing or dying. This need to grow constantly is a positive attribute. What would life be if we were not experiencing the magic of growing constantly? Through the medium of this book, we shine a light on the subtle yet life-altering difference between growing mindfully and growing mindlessly.

At our core, we believe in the paramount importance of being fully connected with our inner selves, our essential nature, and charting our journeys guided by this compass. We believe in the power and magic of intuition as our truest guide to follow. We also believe in the power and magic of operating in a fearless world, or in a space of total freedom, without anything or anybody holding us back from our flight to discover the joys and virtues of our journey.

This is going to be a journey where, together, we will transcend the material web and move towards living a purposeful life in free space.

The Pyramid of Urban Growth

In a typical urban setting, you would find three kinds of species.

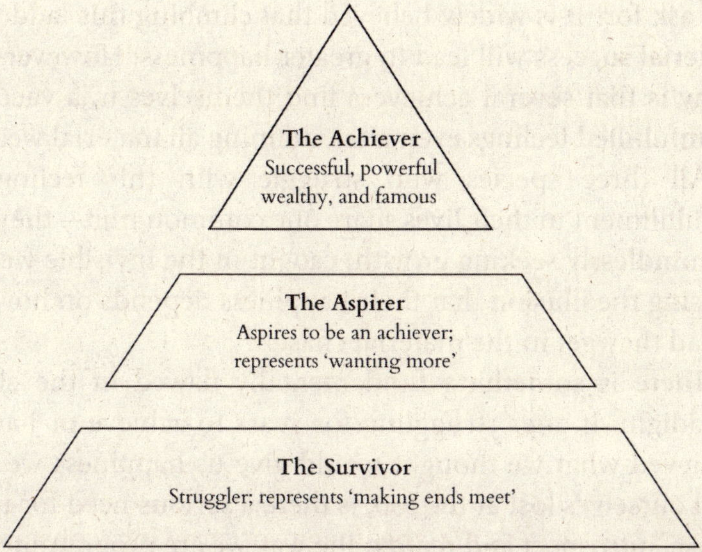

At the base of the pyramid lies 'The Survivors', engaged in a fundamental struggle for survival. For this lot, there is a hunger to grow; however, making basic ends meet is a struggle. As a result, they tend to be need-focused to address their primary requirements first. The hunger to grow keeps the survivors on a mission to reach the pedestal of common recognition.

The second step in this pyramid is a stage where one can truly aspire to achieve something. 'The Aspirers' have taken care of their primary needs and are now in a long-drawn-out chase for more material gains on all fronts—professional, social, and, most importantly, financial.

At the pinnacle of this pyramid is the final set of people who are regarded as gods. They possess power, abundance, and prosperity. They are known as 'The Achievers'. This represents the ultimate goal for everyone pursuing material success. They seem to have pots full of everything a human can ask for! It is widely believed that climbing this ladder of material success will lead to greater happiness. However, the irony is that several achievers find themselves in a vacuum of unfulfilled feelings even after attaining all material wealth.

All three species who struggle with this feeling of unfulfillment in their lives share one common trait—they are all mindlessly seeking growth, caught in the invisible web of chasing the illusion that their happiness depends on how far ahead they get in the material chase.

There is something fundamentally flawed in the chase paradigm. If after struggling for years to achieve or having achieved what we thought would give us happiness we still find ourselves lost at the top, is there a serious need for us to pause, introspect and realign the way we are programmed?

Our parents, friends, religion, environment, and society deeply influence our programming. This is known as 'The Phenomena of Caged Living', where we unconsciously compare every thought, decision, and behaviour to a set of expectations based on norms.

Human beings are born free. In our formative years, we move from being free-thinking and feeling individuals to caged beings. We are confined by our conditioned minds. We are forced to follow the herd or live a life the external influences have led us to believe is the best. The illusion of constantly chasing desires or dreams, rooted in programmed thinking rather than following an inner calling, is where our journeys go wrong.

We often hear stories where people switched careers to make surprisingly different choices. An engineer wakes up one day and decides to become a musician, or a banker quits his job to pursue his love for yoga. We are hearing more and more of such stories today because people are waking up to their inner truth and creating a purposeful life. These are the smarter ones who have become aware that the outside world inspired their choices and the chosen direction was not their own. However, they had the courage and opportunity to redesign their lives and free themselves from the prison of restricted living. They decided to surrender to the soul and not to external conditioning.

We are also increasingly hearing stories where people are gripped with fear and anxiety, have distressed lifestyles, are in meaningless relationships, have an unexplainable emptiness within, struggle with a lack of purpose or self-worth, and suffer from several health complications. These are just some symptoms that push people to look for soul-utions in their lives. These soul-utions may call for a drastic do over or people might create a purpose parallel to their existing occupation, leading to a sustained state of fulfilment.

These stories indicate the emerging need to have the freedom to do and be, to seek inward soul-utions to live a more meaningful life. It is also indicative of a growing desire to love yourself unabashedly. This love for oneself drives our intentions, which then permeates into how we engage with both the physical and invisible spirit world.

It is never too late. You could be at any stage in your life to add the Sanyaas dimension. The fortunate ones will get there earlier. *Sanyaas in the City* is that enabler that can get you on the path to connect with the most real version of you, helping you strip away the masks and versions of yourself you show to the world and, sometimes, to yourself. It's about cultivating an awareness of where the outside influences need to end and where your true calling must take over. In other words, it is about relooking at the fundamental realities that have shaped your journey and exploring the infinite possibilities of living and growing in a world fuelled by your nature. The micro and macro tools can help re-engineer the unconscious programming that has taken you from cradle to cage. This will hopefully help you reverse that process and take you back to Source.

As you grow in your power, you will get into a 'citizen' state of mind. In this state, the chaos and drama of your day-to-day life will no longer influence you, allowing you to flow like a river through the dualities and extreme emotional experiences of your life. To achieve this, you may need to unlearn certain ideas you have picked up along the way. Approach this process with an open mind and commit yourself to connecting deeply with your greatest ally—yourself.

2

Spiritual Awakening: Finding True Freedom

'Just as a candle cannot burn without fire, men cannot live without a spiritual life.'

—Buddha

Life on Earth has been an ongoing phenomenon for millions of years with one constant—evolution. We have witnessed the evolution from the times of the Neanderthals to the farming revolution, the industrial revolution, and now, the massive move towards technology-driven urbanisation. The quest for material gain is the common thread driving humanity through these phases. So powerful is this man-made god of materialism that it has led us from being intrinsically connected beings to outwardly attracted ones.

In our current times, to what extent would you say that our happiness or purpose is reliant on material gain? Even a brief look at the culture that surrounds us suggests that, for many, the two are largely dependent. Why else, for instance, would commercials for luxury cars or perfumes be so aspirational? Is it not for the promise they offer of the 'ideal life' that resonates with a large portion of society? Why else are the lives of city achievers like celebrities, superstars and high-net-worth individuals so endlessly speculated upon?

As we lust for these aspirations, we are conditioned to believe that to be successful and happy is, precisely, to be that person in the Ferrari advert or the cover of a celebrity magazine or on a thumbnail of a highly followed digital offering. Consequently, it becomes only too natural to assume that achieving that image is the ultimate purpose that one can strive towards.

The Invisible Virus: Urban Mind Syndrome (UMS)

The multidimensional information overload constantly pushes us into the allure of material fulfilment where our belief systems and choices are being dictated by herd thinking. From early childhood, our minds sponge in imprints from all fronts—parents, society, religion, and social media. In an urban environment, the density and intensity of impressions and influences cement the view of material chase. This pursuit becomes such a guiding force in our lives that we associate our self-worth with where we stand on the ladder of material evolution. Think about it—even our conversations and relationships with people are engineered around the material index. We are often asked the question: What do you do? Where do you live? On one hand, we are assessing where a person stands on the material index, and on the other hand, we constantly benchmark our aspirations against this index. In a nutshell, whether you are a city achiever, aspirer, or survivor, you may have consciously or unconsciously contracted the syndrome.

Despite the obvious and appealing gravitation towards chasing material success, it is easy to see why doing so can be disappointing. What will we do once we have achieved these things? An hour of the day spent commuting may be replaced with an hour driving through the Tuscan countryside, or you may receive a confidence boost because the paparazzi cannot get enough of you. However, at the most basic level, our day-to-day—or even second-to-second—inner human experience will remain the same. Whether super rich or poor, the fundamental human experience does not change. People on both sides of the equation need to breathe, eat, sleep, and love to get by. The need for life-sustaining actions will remain constant despite where one is on the index.

We must first focus on where our human experience stems from—is it from the inner corridors of knowingness or the external glitz of *Maya* (illusion)? Are we then implying that materialism is always bad? Let us explore this further.

The Spectrum of Materialism

Materialism is a necessity in the real world. A certain degree of it is required for a fulfilling life. Every living being aspires to a good life where we don't have to worry about meeting our basic needs. Beyond the essentials, we all aspire to be able to indulge in pleasurable activities. We need money for everything we want to do in this real world. It is good to have a material outlook; however, it should be a result of doing what you love. Is material lust your main ambition, or are you guided by inner truth and mindful action to attract material abundance? This is the question you need to answer.

Based on how you respond to the question above, you can identify where you stand on the spectrum of materialism.

Mindless Materialist	Mindful Materialist
Purpose: Gaining material	Creating your purpose by doing what you love
Egoistic	Humble/humane
Ruthless	Compassionate
Individualistic: Focused on the I and Me	Inclusive: Focused on the we and thee
Attachment to reward	Focus on action with surrender
Disconnected with your essential nature	Connected with your core
Relationships driven by selfish interests	Relationships driven by love and meaning
Fabricated flow: Outward driven	Intuitive Flow: Driven from within

The I or ego state, this overt identification with our physicality, name, and status, is grounded in materialism. This can lead us towards mindlessness. A mindful way of life is based on the principle of love, as opposed to ego. Journeys founded on the principle of love radically change our outward actions. We apply the love principle to everything we do, everyone we interact with, and, most importantly, how we view and care for ourselves.

In a mindful mindset, we move in the direction of our natural flow, which dictates what we pursue in life. This journey ceases to feel like a job, as we enjoy every moment of walking this path. We can spend hours and days completely immersed, with colossal passion, in creating and doing what excites us from within. The generation of material wealth in this approach is the natural flow of money. The amount of money made should be accepted with grace and used to get by, indulge, and give back. Feel free to apply the one-life principle to the way you spend. Also, remember that giving back is extremely satisfying.

People driven by either the mindless or mindful mindset will use that filter in all aspects of their lives. If you wear green-tinted sunglasses, everything you see will look green. By this simple logic, your material mindset will not only be limited to professional pursuits but also trickle into the quality of your relationships and every other aspect of life.

Let us take a closer look at the effects of materialism on relationships. If the intent behind forming new relationships is driven by materially motivated selfish interests, then these relationships are fundamentally fragile and can crack over time. These relationships are driven by the quest to climb and are flawed at the core.

A mindful materialist, on the other hand, will approach relationships differently. Their connections will have love at the core and move towards being meaningful and nurturing. This is not to say that they will not experience negative relationships. However, they will find intelligent ways of navigating their path out of such relationships, learning from the experience. A mindful materialist will seek more relationships with people who enrich their human experience or help give back.

Wherever you are on the spectrum, between mindless and mindful journeys, you can always choose to move up the ladder of mindfulness to add more value to your life.

First Taste of Freedom

Take a moment to think about the most cherished moments in your life thus far. It might be getting into your dream college, landing your ideal job, or meeting your life partner. Now ask yourself: Why did this moment become the most cherished one in my life? The answer invariably will be in the direction of fulfilling something you deeply desire. Ask yourself another question: How did you feel after achieving these milestones? The answer will possibly be a short-lived feeling of liberation followed by the need to chase something new again.

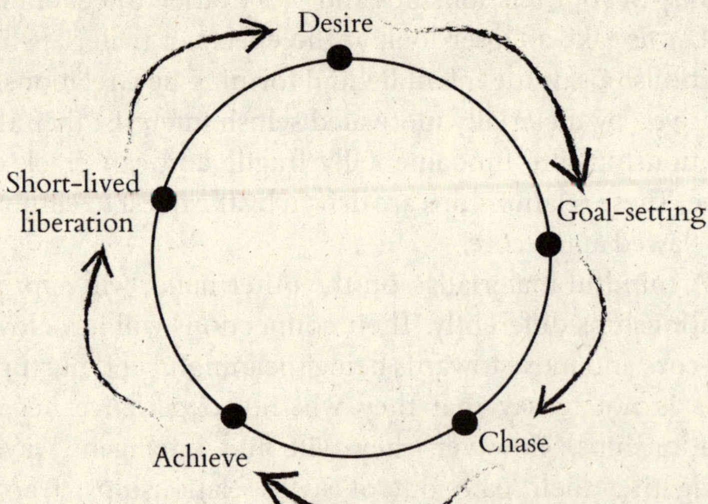

The Freedom Cycle

This short-lived liberation is your first taste of freedom. Liberation of the mind is the most credible reason for our never-ending need to chase newer goals. We are programmed to desire, set goals, achieve, and celebrate in a never-ending loop. Take a minute to observe your life and see if this statement applies to you. In most cases, you will find yourself stuck in this loop.

We keep moving between our primary and secondary desires and chasing that short-lived feeling of liberation. This illusionary loop of chasing desires uproots us from our real selves, locking us in a prison. We move from one cage to the other without even realising it. The cages may get fancier, but they are still cages.

This is a pattern where you toil for years to reach the point of short-lived liberation and are back to chasing something new again. What if there were a way to live where the feeling of liberation or freedom was more sustained and not short-lived? Most of us would eagerly seize this opportunity to live such a life. The truth is, living this liberated life is possible with some fundamental adjustments that most of us can make.

The aim is to transition from mindless materialism to a more enriching, mindful journey. This journey is fuelled by your real nature, rather than chasing the game that most play, which involves accumulating more material at any cost. Desires are not bad; both the mindless and the mindful materialist will have desires. It is the intent behind the desire and the varying levels of attachment to it that can lead to drastically different journeys and outcomes.

Mindful materialism does not mean withdrawing from worldly activities or ambitions. It is about engaging with the world and creating a meaningful purpose from a space of no attachment and total commitment to your unique creation. When you are on a path to creating a meaningful purpose, you can be doggedly driven in how you chart your path to get there. The journey may be taxing, and you may experience phases of extreme pressure and lulls that test your faith. However, you must maintain unwavering faith in the process.

We understand that this bit of writing might seem theoretical at this stage. However, once you have had a chance to read through and implement the practical tools detailed later in the book, you will find the route to achieving this state.

Freedom

Freedom, as the word suggests, is the ultimate state to be—where there is nothing that holds us back from anything. At their core, humans have this instinct to feel free—free of benchmarks or chase, free of the control our mind has over us, free to do things that come naturally, and free to float into newer directions as we grow.

If we observe babies, the first attribute that catches our attention is the sense of freedom in all their activities. The life of a child is free of baggage. They naturally flow from an instant-to-instant basis. If the stimulus is positive, they tend to be happy and vice versa. They have this uncanny ability to get back to the state of peace from either side of the emotional spectrum quickly. They are not tuned to bring the baggage of any memory or the worry of the future into the equation. They live in the moment. When we witness babies engage with life, we notice how the soul beautifully drives their curiosity and actions. In the early stages, their mind is still developing and doesn't possess that kind of power over the human experience. Only when the child grows older does the mind overtake the soul's call.

To feel free, our Soul Mind needs to dominate over other external or Body Mind-triggered impulses. Our human experience should be guided by the power of the soul. We should strive to return to a state of being, doing, and flowing, similar to that of a baby.

Soul Power Flourishes in Free Space

Whilst we may aspire to be free, the reality is that we let worldly pressures take charge of our lives. Such is the power of the world we live in. Allow yourself a moment to introspect, and let yourself accept the weight of these worldly burdens that have managed to creep into your mind. Think about how these unnecessary burdens restrict our path towards the state of freeness.

We must understand that we are not meant to live with this feeling of being continuously weighed down. We might have unconsciously been robbed of our most fundamental right to be and feel free.

Now imagine the possibility of being able to change the course of your life to fly in the direction of your dreams. In this free world, fears dissolve into deep faith, intuition dominates overplanning, and the soul leads ahead of the mind. There is nothing that holds you back from anything.

This paradigm of 'soul power flourishes in free space' has the potential to be a revolution. Like all good things, this, too, has the power to build a new world of no bondage or limitations. A world full of people connected with their nature and in tune with their consciousness. What if there was a world where the majority lived in free space and collective soul power flourished? Isn't this the kind of place we would love to live in?

A quick look at the world at large today tells us a different story. Most countries are driven by this undying need to grow their GDP. The richer countries are all about dominance based on the power of money and military might. The only exception to this mad chase is seen in this small country called Bhutan.

The moment we think of Bhutan, we think of happiness. Bhutan has pegged happiness as a key metric to assess their country's performance, as they have prioritised their Gross National Happiness (GNH).

GNH is a holistic approach to development that aims to balance material and non-material values in the pursuit of happiness. It considers factors such as material security, equitable living standards, and ecological diversity as essential components of well-rounded development. GNH's multidimensional and interconnected nature distinguishes it from GDP as a measure of a country's progress.

Imagine the contrast between living in a place like Bhutan and a hyperactive city like New York. Bhutan thrives on the vitamin of happiness and contentment whereas New York thrives on the virus of materialism. The New York environment is naturally predisposed to building fears at an early stage.. This environment constantly adds newer layers of fear as we grow. On the contrary, Bhutan encourages you to prioritise holistic well-being and happiness above typical material pursuits. The beauty of Bhutan's model is this sentiment is in the air; the entire country breathes this air. The collective manifestation of this quest to strive for happiness ensures that it becomes the primary pursuit for most people growing up in this environment.

This comparison moves in the direction of clarifying that human evolution is a direct result of our environment. Is it possible for us to create a Bhutanese mindscape in the hustle and bustle of a city like New York? Yes, it is!

We endeavour to help you move from the unrelenting chase mindset to a fulfilling and mindful Bhutanese way of life, wherever you might be.

Freeness Visualisation

Experiencing is the best way of learning. This simple visualisation exercise will help you feel light and easy. Find a comfortable spot and guide yourself through this visualisation. This exercise will provide insight into the concept of freedom:

a. Visualise floating on your back in the open waters, looking up at the skies.
b. Consciously free your mind from the burden of the weight of worldly pressures . . . let it go.
c. Experience your body and mind naturally unwinding and surrendering to the bed of water beneath you. Drift with the gentle flow of the tide.
d. As you float and gaze at the expansive skies, experience that feeling of weightlessness.
e. Now bring your attention to the amount of free space you witness between your eyes and the limitless skies.
f. Imagine the infinite number of possibilities in this free space. The beauty of creating your original masterpiece in free space.

g. Having potentially understood the potency of this state of freeness, determine from this point on to chart your journey from material to freedom.

Find Your Balance

Having given you a glimpse of the world of materialism and freedom, it is time to understand this middle path of balance between these two ends. We understand the challenges of a typical city dweller and the difficult act of working through the vital parameters that come into play—getting overdrawn in work, a demanding family life and household responsibilities, the tug of social commitments, and the constant need to achieve material success. This is the whirlpool that most of us find ourselves in at some point in our lives. All discussions between peers and friends circle these issues. We almost start to believe that *this* is the reality of living in a stressful city environment . . . the city truth.

We lose our sense of balance. Everything we have mentioned above is so consuming that most people feel there is no room to mend this pattern. This whirlpool of parameters is why many of us gain weight and suffer from mental health issues. This is also why we are unable to do what we truly want. We have no one else but ourselves to blame for our woes. Resigning to our fate when things are going downhill is not the way to go as this fate can be reversed completely. It starts with introducing some constructive layers to how we live and think.

Let us try to understand this position of living a balanced and peaceful life full of purpose alongside the typical parameters in which we usually find ourselves trapped. This is best explained by looking at the real-life examples of Ratan Tata or Oprah Winfrey. The first thing that comes to mind when we think of these eminent personalities is: Extreme success with a strong human side. They have created multi-billion-dollar empires yet are seen as completely grounded and loving people. They are also known to have given back with full hearts. They epitomise being balanced, successful, and mindful materialists.

We encourage you to move towards freedom, but the extent of your journey is for you to decide. For most of us, the answer is usually found in striking a balance.

To help you get on this path, we will look at balancing the important parameters of our urban compulsions with soul-utions from free space. We will also explore creating balance in all the key aspects of our lives. These aspects will cover everything from finding a balance in choosing what we do to finding our partner, looking after ourselves, choosing our relationships, and finding the balance between working the outside world and growing from the inside.

Is this possible given the mess we find ourselves in at various points in life? Absolutely!

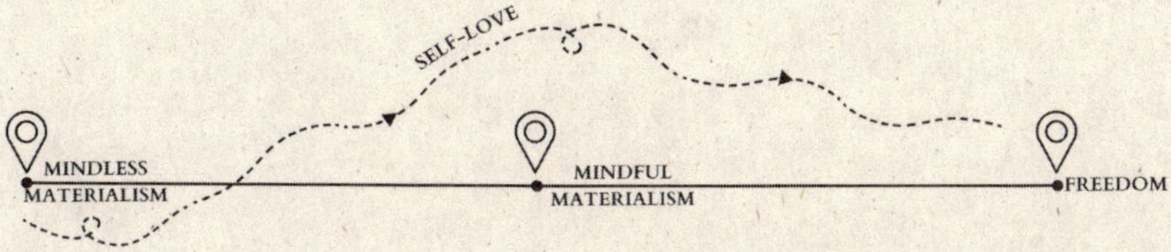

Road to Freedom

The process is simple. The journey begins by first being self-aware of where we stand on the spectrum between mindless materialism and freedom. Self-love is the key to our movement towards living in freeness. By elevating our awareness, we can come to terms with our deviations from our true nature and understand the extent of the depletion in our love energy. We don't need to strive for freedom; we will naturally stumble upon this feeling through our journey of self-love. It is 100 per cent achievable!

3
Self-Awareness

'All the wonders you seek are within yourself.'
—Thomas Browne

Imagine waking up one day and being handed a cancer diagnosis by the doctor. In such a situation, most of us ask ourselves: What will happen to me now? Why did this happen to me? Where did I go wrong? What could I have done differently?

The truth is, it might be too late to ask ourselves such questions. We could have prevented such an outcome had we taken charge of our lives earlier. Why wait for such a drastic incident to realise the importance of living life consciously?

The fact that our source code or our soul's nature is pure love highlights the monumental importance of love in our lives. The amount of love within ourselves radiates outwards, influencing our relationships and interactions with everything and everyone. In other words, the love we give reflects the love we have within.

We come into this world in soul form, which is love, and leave in the soul form. It is during our years on Earth that this pure love nucleus becomes vitiated. A quick look at the soul's life from this perspective will help us discern the need to stay in our pure form of being and operate from a state of love.

Love is the most important factor that determines the quality and experience of our lives. It shapes our leaning towards mindful or mindless materialism. The higher our dependency on love that emanates from within, the more mindful we naturally will be and vice versa. To sum it up, we need to focus on staying on the course of love.

Understanding where we truly stand on the spectrum between material and freedom is the starting point of finding our balance. The objective of our journey to freedom is to build on our fundamental belief that the state of Sanyaas can be achieved wherever we are, with some fundamental fixes.

We need to put brakes on the programmed mind, much like putting brakes on a speeding vehicle approaching an obstacle. It is essential to understand that our deviation from our true nature starts with the programming we are subjected to in our early years. We also need to recognise that this programming depletes our natural state of being 100 per cent love. Depending on the environment we are exposed to, our love for ourselves can range between one and a hundred on the index.

It is essential to comprehend that our actions and behaviour are a direct result of the extent of depletion from our love centre. Below is a self-assessment exercise that will help you understand the level of depletion you might have been operating from over the years.

When life is on a roll for most of us, it is challenging to make drastic changes. However, if we understand the importance of this one decision to assess where we stand and how it will impact the rest of our lives, it makes it worth considering.

Do you remember the first few days at school when we had no idea what to expect from new classes, yet the entire experience was designed to make the interaction absorbing and fun, leaving behind solid impressions to grow? Try to apply the same filter as we get you in the mood for an exercise.

To know where you need to go, it is crucial to realise where you are. We have devised a simple yet effective self-awareness tool to help you take stock of ground zero and find where you stand on the spectrum. If you are leaning towards caged living, your love centre will naturally be in depletion mode, and you may be potentially running low on your vitamin love levels. However, if you score closer to freedom, you are naturally functioning from a fuller love centre.

The Material Index

Once you have identified where you are, you can start a parallel journey to your existing one where we will guide you to connect with your love hub or your real self. The rest is a marvel of synchronicity waiting to unfold.

Let us start by answering honestly to the inner enquiries listed below. Your responses need to be rated between 1 and 5.

1 – Strongly disagree; 2 – Disagree; 3 – Neutral;
4 – Agree; 5 – Strongly agree

1. Making money is the primary goal of my life.
2. I lust for position and power.
3. I am hungry to grow in my social stature. I want to hobnob with the A-listers.
4. I am willing to overstep and cross boundaries to make money.
5. My health is suffering because I am pushing myself too hard at work.
6. I feel increasingly stressed in my day-to-day life.
7. I gravitate towards people from whom I can benefit.
8. I find myself comparing my growth and worth with others.
9. I am naturally predisposed to seeking love from others to feel happy.
10. I want to control the future of my children.
11. I am more focused on what I am receiving vis-à-vis what I have to offer.
12. I worry too much about the past or the future.
13. My self-worth is defined by my net worth.
14. I am compelled to prove to others that I am always right.
15. I am deeply attached to the reward of my actions.

16. My brand of house, car, and other possessions determine my status.
17. I judge others based on the kind of house or car they own.
18. I need to control every aspect of my life.
19. I am overly attached to my desires.
20. I can easily fall into the trap of unhealthy living.
21. I am prone to stress-eating.
22. I have sleep issues.
23. Smoking, drinking, or narcotics help me cope with stress.
24. I like meaningless casual sex.
25. My social media image is important.
26. I am prone to letting my ego get in the way of my relationships and dealings.
27. I have strong feelings of hate and jealousy.
28. I am extremely fearful of losing my savings.
29. I feel there is nothing wrong with exploiting our environment for economic well-being.
30. I do not feel the need to spend time with nature.
31. Money drives all my actions and relationships.
32. I do not believe in a higher power that guides us.
33. I do not believe in there being a synchronistic design to realising my dreams.
34. I conform to societal and/or religious norms and guidelines.
35. Mindfulness doesn't come to me naturally.
36. I prioritise loving others before loving myself.

37. I am more focused on appearance than substance.
38. I feel like I do not have a strong purpose to live and give back.
39. I cannot connect with my intuition.
40. I experience negative emotions regularly.
41. I find it difficult to forgive and move on.
42. I cannot witness the events in my life without attachment.
43. I attach an expectation from all my actions.
44. I don't believe in the existence of a soul.
45. I struggle to bounce back from adversity in quick time.
46. I cannot live in the moment.
47. I worry about what people think about me.
48. I fear death.
49. I cannot prioritise my physical and mental well-being.
50. I don't like being alone.

Your score on this evaluation is the sum of all individual responses and can range between 50 and 250. The closer your score is towards 50, the closer you are towards feeling free. If your score is leaning towards 250, consider yourself in the firm grip of mindless materialism.

We want to, once again, remind you that this score of self-assessment also reflects the extent of depletion or fullness of your love centre. As explained earlier, our manifestations mentioned in the assessment above stem from the state of our love hub. We have assigned a 'Vitamin Love Index' to help you understand the extent of your departure from your true nature which is 100 per cent love.

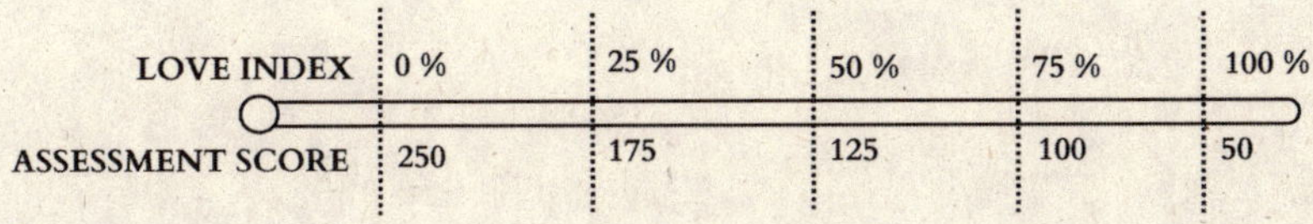

Vitamin Love Index

Note: This method of scoring is simply meant to give you a broad understanding of your deviation from your core, and the score is to be treated only as an indicative metric.

Feel free to run through this exercise at various points in your journey from this point on and map your scores to see how you are travelling. A lot of us, in all honesty, would rate more in the direction of being material-minded. Visualise yourself being stuck underwater with water being the equivalent of material. We will help you raise your head, that is raise your awareness, to be able to get out of the water and breathe.

Imagine the feeling when you move from feeling breathless underwater to being able to breathe freely. Welcome to the world of love!

4

Barriers to Freedom

'If you play without the shackles and burdens, then you play like you did when you were a kid.'

—Robert Green

Multiple potential issues can hold you back, stunting your journey towards living in a free space. Recognising these barriers to freedom is the first step towards liberation.

Honest introspection will help you identify the real thieves of your freedom. This involves spending time in deep thought to unravel the real culprits. It is through this quest that you gain clarity, which, in turn, helps you deal with these thieves accordingly.

We have identified four categories of potential zones that can rob us of our right to live freely. This framework of the four zones will aid you during your phases of introspection. These zones progress from gross physical levels to more subtle planes and directly reflect our depleted love centre. The degree of depletion determines the intensity with which these barriers influence our lives.

We must keep an open mind to comprehend the more subtle planes as they extend beyond physicality into abstract themes. The key is to keep an open mind throughout.

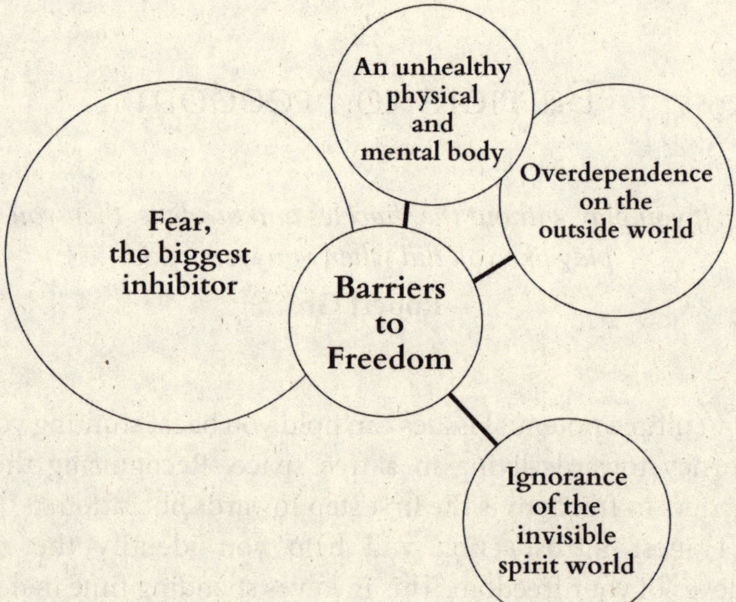

Barriers to Freedom

Fear: The Biggest Inhibitor

If we had to point out one major obstacle that inhibits our movement towards freedom and happiness, it would be fear. Fear can manifest in various forms and levels, both physical and mental, such as fear of failure, physical harm, rejection, loneliness, and death.

Death is the most powerful fear experienced by humans, and if we could find a way to make friends with this fear, perhaps, nothing else would worry us as much. The fear of death enters our journey typically during the middle years when we hear about the isolated incidents of people from our peer group dying before their time. We can relate to death as we witness it happening to someone in our age bracket. The thought that '*this could happen to me*' intimidates us, leading to the idea of death entering our conscious minds. This fear grows as the years pass and we hear of more people in our peer group passing away. In the hierarchy of our fears, death becomes the greatest concern.

For some, it begins the process of natural realignment to finding the real answers and creating a more meaningful life. However, for most, it sits there as a fear marker, subconsciously driving a more fatalistic mindset. Given the inevitable nature of death, this lot of people live with the principle of wanting to make the most of this life, even if it treads on mindlessness. They want to take on big debts to live the big life, eat like there is no tomorrow, and indulge in all the excesses that accompany the desire to live life to the fullest. This craving to live life mindlessly to the fullest is where the fatalists go astray. Since they are driven by the Body Mind, death remains their biggest fear. Their love for life is so overwhelming that any potential threat to it is incomprehensible.

At a gross level, we identify life with the body, associating it with form and physicality. Death is simply moving out of the body into a subtler dimension of being formless and non-physical. Once we understand that through death, we are relinquishing the garment of the body to pass into a formless and invisible state, we can change our perception of death from being the end to a point of transition.

Our ego makes us fear death, leading to the fear of losing consciousness, identity, and physicality. The ego cannot embrace death. When we dissolve the influence of the ego mind and think and feel consciously from the Soul Mind, we transform our relationship with death. From the Soul Mind, we do not fear death, instead, we view it as a part of our ongoing journey and may even look forward to this new experience as an adventure.

Most individuals who have faced a near-death experience describe it as blissful. Some often express that their experience on the side of death was so profound that they did not want to return to life.

The journey after death is a function of our karmic actions of the current and previous births. Thus, we are responsible for our post-death destiny. We can potentially change the course of our post-death journey by taking charge of our karmic actions as soon as today. We are on the right track if our current actions are guided by love at the source.

Having understood the reality of our biggest fear of death, let us now understand the other major fear inducers and the truth of them all.

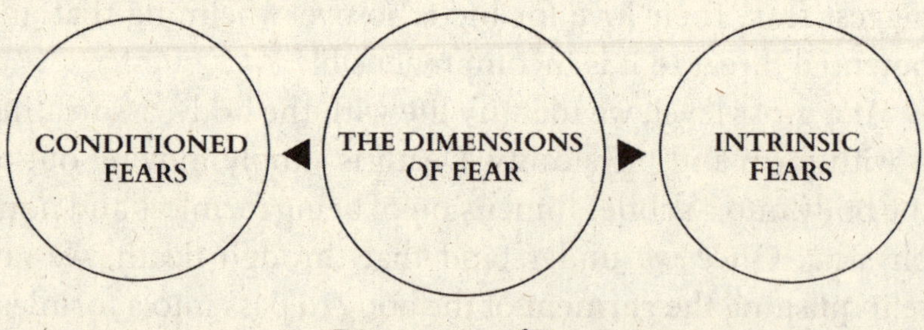

Dimensions of Fear

Upon closer inspection, we can discern that our fears exist in two dimensions—conditioned and intrinsic fears. Conditioned fears are induced by our interactions with the outside world, which we have learnt over time. Parental influence, social programming, expectations, or environmental threats can create a conditioned fear response within us. You might have acquired the fear of failure from the criticism you received for bad grades in school. A pandemic like COVID-19 could have induced the fear of loneliness, disease, or even death. The degree of fear is directly related to how much we have departed from our loving nature and allowed these fears to grow within us. These conditioned fears can be shallow or deeply rooted. If they have taken a spot in our subconscious, overcoming them may be a challenge, but it is still possible.

Intrinsic fears are innate fears that have been hardwired into us. We might be carrying this fear at a DNA level of our soul. These fears start showing up in the early years of our lives. There is no logical reason for these fears to turn up, yet they exist and evoke fearful responses. Take an example of a child at the age of one or two, shrieking at the sight of heights, or another child of the same age who is afraid of water. These intrinsic fears could be the embers of a past life experience. The reasons behind these intrinsic fears might elude us, however, the fact that they exist at a level of our Soul Mind needs to be clearly understood.

Our fears tend to evolve as we grow through different phases of life. In the first phase of life, as children, we display fearlessness when trying new things. For instance, a child learning how to stand doesn't fear falling and makes multiple attempts before s/he can stand comfortably. Does the fear of falling prevent the child from trying to stand again? It does not.

There is a great real-life lesson in this for most of us. A child relates to its true nature of being free and fearless. Remember, we were all there once. As we grow through life, we lose that connection and replace our loving nature with conditioned, fearful thinking. As we begin our never-ending chase, fear takes its permanent position in our minds. The extent of fear and the number of triggers may vary but we all become victims of this great inhibitor. Most people deal with their fears the way they know best; however, fears have this uncanny ability to keep bouncing back with more ferocity.

If we, as intelligent beings, understand the consequences of breeding fear in our minds, why do most of us still allow this to happen?

Recollect an incident where you were fearful of something, and you will find that your fear had a major influence on the choices you ended up making. This is how fear controls us. The ability to manage our fear differentiates the wise from the rest. A person may either completely succumb to it on one extreme and suffer from major medical issues or may end up conquering their fears to write their stories of triumph. Where would you want to be?

Fear management is the key to being closer to love. Fear, like every other emotion, is meant to be experienced. However, we have been programmed to perceive it as a negative emotion. The secret of dealing with fear is to use it in the right measure and for the right reasons. The Soul Mind uses fear as an emotion for growth. The moment we can look at any fear-inducing stimulus and use the Soul Mind to neutralise it, we are mastering it.

The Fear Reflection Exercise

Now that we have understood fear better, we can use this opportunity to reflect on the nature of our relationship with this great inhibitor. Below is a compilation of some common fears experienced by people. This list essentially focuses on the conditioned fears that are induced by the external world. Have you ever experienced any of them? Were you robbed of your experience of life because of the potency of your fear? Or were you able to manage your fear healthily?

Fear of the Unknown	Fear of Losing Material Gains	Fear of Failure	Fear of Not Matching Expectations
Fear of Rejection	Fear of Not Fitting In	Fear of Missing Out	Fear of Discrimination
Fear of Losing a Loved One	Fear of Change	Fear of Financial Insecurity	Fear of Insecurity in Relationships
Fear of Loneliness	Fear of Death	Fear of Old Age	Fear of Responsibility
Fear of Dependence	Fear of Disease	Phobias (objects, animals, places, and space)	Fear of Judgement
Fear of Inadequacy	Fear of Success	Fear of Violence	Fear of Commitment

Use the space below to uncover the fears you may have faced in your journey thus far and their impact on your life. Your fear(s) may or may not be from the above-mentioned list.

We hope you will have clarity on the nature of your fears at this stage. Are you a person who easily gets drawn into fearful thinking or are you someone who has better mind control to manage your fears? It is not uncommon to feel that your fears have got the better of you and brought out the not-so-best in you.

On our path to Sanyaas, one of the prerequisites is to love yourself like crazy. This degree of love is experienced only when you have managed to uproot fear from the core. Later in the book, we will take you through an effective tool, the drain cleansing programme, to help you overcome fears and other negative emotions draining your love centre. Miracles take place only in a free state of mind.

Overdependence on the Outer World

Scientific findings today reveal that a child soaks in conditioning from all sources in their early years of life. This happens unconsciously and forms the blueprint of the child's life journey. As life progresses, we become aware of the creative possibilities of a conscious mind; however, we are unconscious about being run by the conditioning of the formative years. This leads us to experience a robotic life with little room for true self-expression or creativity.

These initial years of our lives lay the trap for us to completely live in the illusory outer world. Later in life, we spend more than 90 per cent of our day working towards the desires that stem from our early conditioning, trying to succeed in the outer world. This becomes our absolute truth, inheriting this practical or logical world and being bound by it.

We drift in the direction of becoming victims of science and logic. We refuse to believe in anything that is not scientifically proven, struggle to relate to anything that does not stand the test of logic, and cage ourselves in the world of space-time or the outer world, losing sight of the principles of freeness and love.

Our self-perception relies strongly on our physicality, thoughts, and emotions. This sense of I is called ego. The ego becomes that invisible filter with which we interact and perceive the world. We live this life with an absolute belief in this identity. We describe the outer world as the relationship between 'I' and everything that 'I' interacts with, which includes people, nature, and everything material—both tangible and intangible.

While we need to use this vital aspect of our personification to survive, it is important to differentiate between mindful and mindless ego. When our existence is heavily dependent on the outer world, we are in the firm grip of mindless ego. The most relatable situations that many of us encounter and fall in love with include gaining wealth and longing for more, gaining love and longing for more, and gaining recognition and longing for more. We internalise this paradigm and cannot imagine life without these external plug-ins. Any disruption to this pattern leaves us in shreds.

The stockpile of impressions leading us to this destiny is based on the fundamental falsehood of believing in the concept of us being limited to our bodies, us being the 'doers', and material being the ultimate God. We end up creating a false identity based on our ego. Before we realise it, we become subservient to this identity, thereby losing our true selves somewhere along the way. We can spend an entire lifetime trapped in this mindless ego way of life.

In the process of gaining material heights, we start to rely on this outer world so much that we relinquish our power. We build our self-image based on what people think of us and how much material wealth we possess. We also get affected by what others say about us and how they treat us.

'If I have scaled big brand positions, I am on the fast track to success. If I am seen driving a fancy car, I have made it in the eyes of people. If I mingle with socially coveted people, I am in the right league.' These thoughts emerge from a mindless ego state. Have we ever sat back and paid attention to why these kinds of thoughts enter our minds? Why is there a need to feel a sense of self-worth based on validation from the external world? We are so consumed by our chase that we lose track of the fundamentals. We start to live and grow in our minds according to how the world perceives us, which eventually leads to a vacuum within us. This is the gap between who we truly are and what we have chosen to become.

Seeking love in relationships is another important aspect of our lives where we are overdependent on the outside world. Why do we feel the need to feel good about ourselves based on how much people love us?

The paradox of love is what we need to understand. When we seek love, it eludes us. The more we desire it, the more we are susceptible to experiencing waves of disappointment and disillusionment. When we stop seeking and depending on the outside world for love and nurture our love centre within, we slowly move in the direction of becoming love ourselves. When we radiate that love energy, we attract and manifest it effortlessly in our lives. What we try and achieve with effort and rejection comes our way organically when we are soaked in love ourselves. *Be* love, do not seek it.

The reality is that at some point or the other, we wake up to this beautiful realisation that our belief system of looking outwards for happiness was fundamentally flawed. We realise that we are indeed our best friends and confidants and can find the deepest reservoirs of happiness and fulfilment and answers within. It is important to engage with the outer world with this truth that eventually the answers will be found within us, nowhere else.

When looked at from the mind of our soul, the outer world is the world of illusion. This world presents an opportunity to experience a transient phase of our lives without attachment. Phases of the highs and lows, growth and falls, love and hate are all fleeting. The only constant is the mind of the soul, helping us use our ego more mindfully.

Mindful ego is an interesting facet of our identity that we need to use to get by. This is a mind state that allows us to navigate through life confidently, assertively, and empathetically while maintaining a realistic view of ourselves. This is a mind state where we are aware of this facet called ego and use it to interact with the world maturely. The important difference is that we use it consciously instead of being controlled by it. The moment we look at what ego does to our life from a distance, we can take stock of the fallout and damage of its mindless use.

We want to share an interesting self-introspection exercise that we can run for ourselves to understand the impact of living the mindless ego life.

Make a list of all the vital decisions in your life and observe how your ego influenced the decisions. Discern between the use of mindless or mindful ego. When you look at the list of decisions taken from a mindless ego state, you will be able to see the ramifications that unfolded clearly.

Key Decisions	Were they driven by a mindful or mindless ego state?	What were the ramifications of functioning from a mindless ego state?

An Unhealthy Physical and Mental Body

In our sunshine years, looking after ourselves is not a priority. The focus is more on external achievements rather than inner well-being. At this stage, we tend to think from the Body

Mind, becoming consumed by aspirations for professional advancement, financial stability, and social recognition. Consequently, self-care is often neglected.

Our relentless quest for material growth takes a toll on our physical and mental bodies, inhibiting us from experiencing true freedom. Neglecting our well-being for external pursuits creates an imbalance, leading to stress and disease. What is the worth of wealth, name, or fame if it comes at the cost of our ability to enjoy it in good health? Unfortunately, most of us only wake up to this realisation when we experience a negative event.

In a state of Soul Mind thinking, we are conscious of everything. We make choices based on the principles of nature, recognising the need to look after our bodies—mentally, physically, and spiritually. We understand the importance of maintaining our bodies in their natural form to experience freedom to the fullest.

A healthy body often resides in a strong mind, which further requires an awareness of our Soul Mind. A strong mind can be experienced only through the lens of the Soul Mind. With a mind in control, we can adequately care for our physical bodies and fight back when faced with challenges. Above all, a strong mind allows us to stay calm in the worst situations, embodying the mind state of a sanyaasi—clear and resilient.

In the human journey, three pillars determine our overall health: Genetics, lifestyle, and karma. Here is a secret many may not share: These pillars can largely be influenced by the mind of our soul. This means we can significantly shape the journeys of our lives.

The science of Epigenetics reveals that only about 5 per cent of our life is influenced by our genes. The remaining

95 per cent is determined by the environment we live in. The more loving and happier our world is, the more we thrive. Research in Genealogy shows how our surroundings fundamentally affect our bodies.

Epigenetics also emphasises the importance of feeding our bodies with nutritious blood that supports the function of every cell. Our state of mind, along with nutrition and lifestyle, determines the chemical cocktail in our blood. Happy mind states release nourishing chemicals like oxytocin and dopamine, while negative or stress-driven states release toxic chemicals like cortisol, leading to an unhealthy body and mind.

Our bodies consist of trillions of cells, each responding to signals created by our thoughts and emotions. Imagine your body as an energy field influenced by the nature of the energy it receives. We must keep our cells in a happy state. In difficult phases, we experience shocks and aftershocks from unpleasant events. Adding negative emotions to this mix creates a toxic storm. Sanyaas is about witnessing incidents with detachment, changing the direction of the wind instead of dwelling in negativity. We need to consciously condition our minds with positive thoughts, even if things are not back to normal. You will be amazed at the outcome. Positive thinking in negative environments can be akin to a miraculous life-saving drug.

Karma, as we know, is the phenomenon of cause and effect. Every action has an equal and opposite reaction, experienced at some point in this life or another. Many of us hear about karma but believe it doesn't apply to us. This naive thinking changes when we encounter real-life experiences proving otherwise.

Can our karma be managed to stay on the right side? Despite all theories and debates, the answer is simple—stay connected with our love centre. Love in, love out. This mantra positively impacts our karmic equations. Loving ourselves deeply and purely guides us to make decisions from the heart, staying on the right side of karma. Being heart-focused is the gateway to Soul Mind realisation, resulting in a core full of love. Decisions made from this core are often virtuous; those made from the Body Mind have a high chance of being non-aligned.

Lifestyle is our ability to care for our physical and mental bodies as nature intended. Observing someone can tell their lifestyle story. Some in their 20s look old and out of shape, while others in their 60s look vibrant and youthful. Some are dull and negative, while others are radiant and positive. Lifestyle, a controllable parameter, is either used judiciously or ignored. Globally, poor lifestyles have created a thriving medical and pharmaceutical industry. Why should we reach a stage of needing hospitals or medicines when we can maintain our health and minimise medical interventions? The best pharmacy is within our minds and bodies, and we must strive to prioritise self-care along with our other pursuits.

After all, don't we all want to wake up feeling great, ready to tackle the day with energy, doing what we love? Don't we all want to feel free and not caged by a diseased body and mind?

Ignorance of the Invisible Soul World

Ignorance, in this case, is not bliss. Our view of the absolute truth of the physical world, and our unwavering faith in science and logic, limit our potential. We read about the existence of a soul and all the theories surrounding its immortality. However, we look at these claims with a wish that they were true but do not fully believe in them. This feeling of disbelief stems from the lack of scientific proof. The concept of a soul remains a wishful thought.

We are now entering a space similar to outer space in Astronomy—a wonderful world where there exists an ocean of unending information still being comprehended. This is about understanding the subtle difference between what we know as reality and the reality that guides us.

How many times have you sat there, looking up at the stars, wondering what a star would look like up close? Or sitting in a city, feeling as though you were gliding down the slopes of the Alps? This phenomenon of shifting our thoughts or awareness wherever we want is testimony to the fact that our awareness or consciousness is not restricted to our bodily form. This opens a fascinating world beyond the limitations of a mind contained within a physical body.

The moment we make friends with the simple reality that we are much more than our physical bodies, and that consciousness transcends what humans know or comprehend, our world opens to infinite possibilities. Our bodies are confined, but consciousness is limitless. While our minds and bodies are programmed to think within the constraints of space, time, and causation, our consciousness can transcend these and enter timeless, free realms.

Consciousness is directly connected with understanding our soul. Much like the concept of an immortal soul, consciousness, too, is eternal. For simplicity, imagine consciousness as the mind of the soul. Now, we have two dimensions to our being—one of Body Mind, limited to the physical and ego-driven world, and the other of Soul Mind, beyond the physical confines, thriving eternally in a world of love. Here, we realise our higher power, our inner voice, and are guided by it. At the soul's level, we witness without being affected by anyone or anything. We have unwavering faith and trust in our higher power. Our true nature is indeed our higher power or God. In this realisation, we accept everything that comes our way without question, understanding a grand design at play.

Thinking from the Soul Mind is a profoundly transformative concept that can lead to a life of inner purpose and flow in a fearless, open world. For many, the alien and unscientific wisdom of this approach might hold them back from adopting this way of being. We encourage you to explore works by some of the greatest spirit masters, such as Osho and Paramhansa Yogananda, whose commentary on soul truths can deepen your understanding.

At a practical level, we need to take baby steps towards internalising this reality. These steps begin with spending more time alone in meditation, either self-guided or with a mentor, to unlock the doorway to our inward journey. Meditation serves as both the starting point and the medium that can lead us to deep self-realisation and transformation. Continuously feeding our minds with a desire to explore this higher truth, guided by genuine intent, will naturally lead to meditative experiences that help internalise this truth.

5
Self-Love: Discovering the Beauty Within

'Since love grows within you, so beauty grows. For love is the beauty of the soul.'

—Saint Augustine

When the love for our essence is 100 per cent, we are in a state of self-love. As we lose ourselves in the urban matrix of desires, expectations, and the relentless chase for material success, we get completely engrossed in the world and the relationships outside us. This makes us lose sight of the most fundamental truth of our existence—we are the sole experiencers of our body and soul's journey. We enter the world alone and exit it alone as well. We want to celebrate our highs with our near and dear ones and need their support during our lows. The naked truth, however, is that we are the ultimate observers of these phases, in isolation. As the illusion of these ego-fuelled roles entraps us, we fail to prioritise the single most important part of this equation—ourselves.

As we hop on the boat en route to self-love, we discover and embrace our solitary nature. Within this aloneness is a whole world of happiness, bliss, companionship, and answers, guiding us towards freeness. The moment we start our journeys back to where we truly belong, we experience its beauty. Love is the magnet that pulls us more and more towards itself until we become love. Love forms the innermost sheath of our existence, and it is our responsibility to keep our physical journeys of this birth as close to the love nucleus as possible, as that is when we will operate from our true nature.

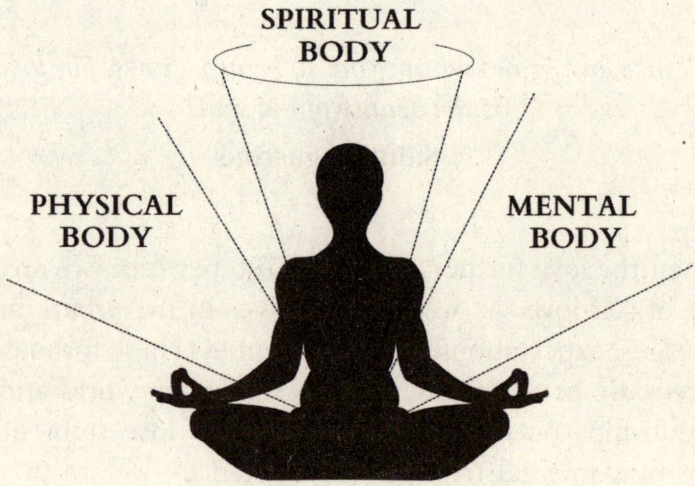

Three Dimensions of the Inner Nucleus

Three distinct dimensions fuel our inner nucleus of love—physicality, mental body, and the most critical invisible dimension of our spirit, the spiritual body. Self-actualisation involves a clear and deep understanding of each of these dimensions. It also includes our committed and consistent effort to stay on course.

Given our circumstances, we might be drawn to any one of these dimensions as the starting point of our journey in the search for our truest love. Our truest love is indeed our deep love for our soul self. As we move on this path with honesty, the yearning for the other two dimensions begins naturally, which eventually helps us discover this divine yet simple secret about our real origin. Any departure from the love nucleus means dissonance in our journey, which we can feel as unease or disease despite having it all.

At the level of our physical, mental, and spiritual selves, many of us experienced this reality during the COVID-19 pandemic. Many lost their lives due to pre-existing comorbidities owing to poor lifestyles. People with preconditions happened to be the most vulnerable to suffering deeply from the consequences of the virus. It was during this phase that the need to prioritise our health and well-being caught steam. We suddenly witnessed a spike in people consciously building their mental resilience, eating right, working out, and seeking the deeper truths of life.

However, why did it take a pandemic for people to understand the need to start loving themselves?

This question leads us to understand the paramount importance of self-love as one's ultimate goal of going through life. In a state of self-love, we effortlessly emanate love from within to the outside world. Simply put, we become loving beings. Our journey of love for the outer layers of our existence begins from the innermost self.

Self-love is sometimes misunderstood. Some might consider this a license to being and acting selfishly. Selfishness is an expression of a depleted or disconnected love centre. Anyone in complete love with oneself would naturally not be selfish, exuding love to everything external, given the multidimensional love nourishment. We are, in fact, encouraging you to love yourself more than anything or anyone else in the world.

When we are on track, we naturally tend to be healthier and wiser. This, in turn, keeps everyone in our inner circle—of family and loved ones—worry-free and at ease. This self-prioritisation is not selfish but strongly motivated by love for ourselves and others. Imagine a family where all members believe in the inherent virtue of being in love with themselves. It would form a perfect foundation for families to live and grow naturally, happily, and healthily.

The experience of loving yourself will make you look better, feel even better, and most importantly, attract naturally. You will transform into the centre point of the mystic attraction called *aakarshan.* It is not about having physically attractive looks; it involves emanating a mystic aura of love that will organically attract others.

This state of *aakarshan* needs to be used responsibly. When you naturally attract others, it becomes your responsibility to give back for universal good and growth.

The Seamless Design of Love

Love has this uncanny habit of seeping through the layers much like the process of osmosis and reverse osmosis. Before you realise it, a dual carriageway falls into place, which sets up the road to inward and outward love.

Let us dive into the insides of this love phenomenon.

At the core of this thought is this beautiful heart called love. The more we love in, the more we love out. As we energise ourselves with this essence of love in its truest and purest form, we will find our heart's essence first radiating outwards in our physical and mental representations, and then beyond. The formula is simple: Stay true to your core

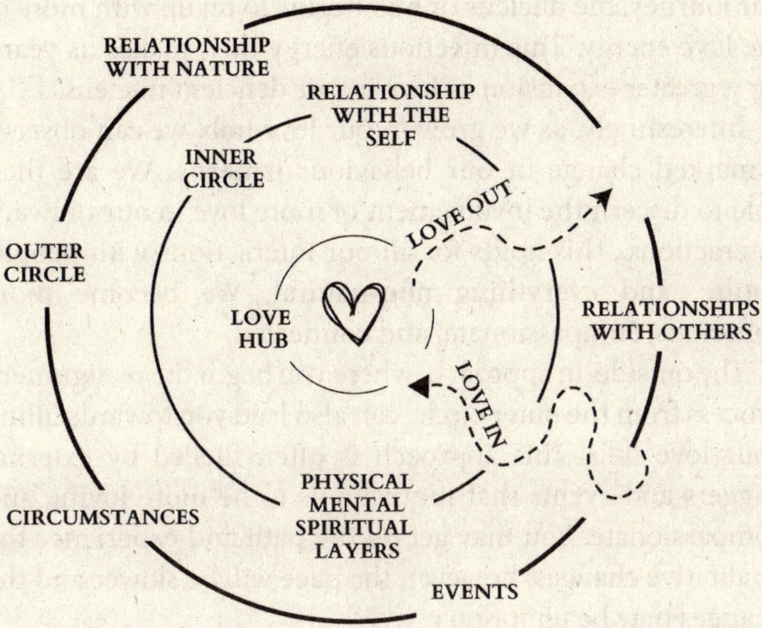

The Love Phenomenon

and the rest gets taken care of. On the contrary, the more we stray from our essence, the more it shows through our outer representations.

This process of realignment works best when it moves from the innermost to the outer circles. The inner circle is our relationship with our physical, mental, and spiritual dimensions, and the outer circle represents our relationship with everything and everybody we experience on an ongoing basis, including our relationship with nature.

We should be aware of our position on the love index based on the self-awareness exercise in Chapter 3. This exercise reveals the extent of depletion of our nucleus. Depending on which dimension of the inner circle we connect with to start our journey, the nucleus or hub begins to fill up with more of the love energy. This infectious energy then makes us yearn for a greater expansion of love in our deficient nucleus.

Interestingly, as we grow in our love hub, we can observe a marked change in our behaviour patterns. We are then able to discern the involvement of more love in our outward interactions. This holds for all our interactions with people, nature, and everything non-natural. We become more conscious, compassionate, and connected.

The outside-in approach, where you begin the realignment process from the outer circle, can also lead you towards filling your love hub. This approach is often fuelled by external triggers and events that motivate us to be more loving and compassionate. You may get on the path and experience the qualitative changes; however, the pace will be slower and the changes may be temporary.

The fastest way to fill your love hub is by making fundamental fixes within the inner circle, which will show through in the outer circle at an unprecedented pace.

6

The Self-Love Toolkit: Essentials for Inner Peace

'To fall in love with yourself is the first secret to happiness.'

—Robert Morley

To help you fall headlong in love with yourself, we have assembled a practical toolkit that addresses all three dimensions of your truth. This set of tools is a comprehensive guide inspired by the science of yoga. This Self-love toolkit will help you start your journey towards experiencing the freedom that stems from filling your love centre.

As they say, most battles are won with a clear mind and resolve. The moment we decide to get on the path with honesty and truth, we can scale any mountain. The starting point of our toolkit will help you internalise this profound truth.

Sankalpa: The Single-Minded Resolve

The ancient Indian epic Mahabharata has multiple beautiful stories that can help us understand the essence of *sankalpa*, which means a single-minded focus. According to one of the stories, Dronacharya, the revered warrior and guru of the royals, was teaching archery to the Pandavas. As a part of the ongoing training, he decided to test the subjects. He hung a wooden bird from a tree and asked each of his students to look at the target—the eye of the bird—and tell him what they could see. Most of their responses included mentions of the bird, the tree, and the surroundings. However, Prince Arjuna came up with the answer Dronacharaya was looking for. Arjuna could only see the eye of the bird and nothing else. Such needs to be the focus and clarity of our intent.

Sankalpa is a Sanskrit term that refers to a deeply held intention or resolution one sets for oneself, often in a spiritual or meditative practice. At the heart of the strategy required to find ourselves is the degree of our focus and the truthfulness of our intent. We must align all our thoughts, actions, and beliefs with our deepest desire to connect with our true selves.

We must have a single-minded resolve to love ourselves to the point of absolute. In this state, we will find all the answers to our questions of origins, such as 'Who am I? What is my purpose? Where do I go post-death?'

This search can be frustrating. The more we force our minds to find the answers, the more the answers will elude us. These answers cannot be pushed out of our systems, as they come to us over time naturally. Do not lose faith or get dejected at any point in this search. The answers will appear if you are truly committed and at moments when you least expect them. Believe in the process, and don't forget to enjoy every moment of this journey. It is important to keep that firm intention alive at the back of your mind and go through the elements of the toolkit with honesty. Hopefully, you will have clarity at the end of this experiential learning journey.

Have faith that your determination and the tools mentioned in this book will help in the process of self-actualisation.

The SITC Method: Intuitive Living

Look around and you will find several methods recommended by the global top experts on movement, nutrition, mental wellness, and spiritual awakening. Who to follow is always a question that leads to confusion. The reason behind this confusion is that we are listening to experts who have built their methods based on specific reference criteria. The best method is always a function of knowing the fundamentals of the subject and creating your methods based on your intuition. This journey of finding the real you must be your very own discovery.

For many of us, intuition guides us every step of the way. For others, it is an abstract concept that is too out there. We have heard of some incredible success stories about people who worked on their intuition and built successful and satisfying legacies. So, what differentiates intuitive people from non-believers?

The answer lies in our true belief in the existence of our soul. When we internalise the presence of the unseen Soul Mind and consider it our real identity, we witness intuitive suggestions at every step of the way. We encounter the law of least effort. This intuition is simply your Soul Mind guiding your Body Mind forward.

As we embark on this journey of self-discovery, we will help you with a structured framework of set routines, guidelines, and core philosophies that you can integrate into your lives. After initially adopting the process and understanding the fundamentals of the subject, you will be able to make intuitive adjustments.

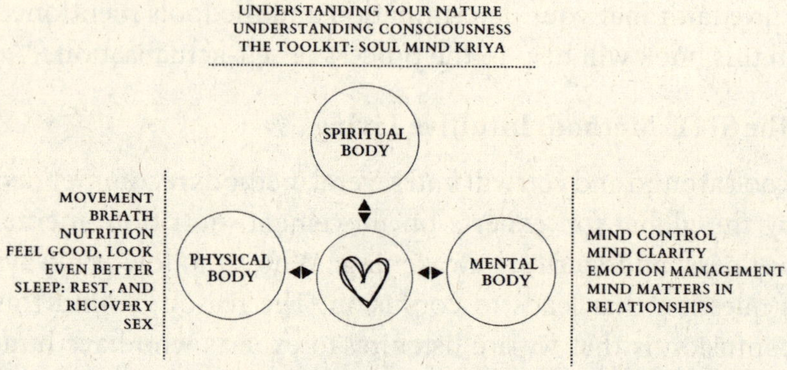

The Self-Love Toolkit

The three pillars of this self-love toolkit involve working on our physical, mental, and spiritual bodies to achieve self-knowingness. Most of us follow methods with a limited focus on either movement, nutrition, emotion management, or the quest for unravelling spiritual truths. The biggest differentiator in our approach is the comprehensiveness of how we need to approach our real selves. We don't solely focus on one or two dimensions of our journey; we truly believe that to realise yourself, the body, mind, and spirit need to work in tandem. You will recognise the uniqueness of this toolkit once you start experiencing the monumental shift that takes place while working on the three dimensions simultaneously.

6.1

Physical Body: The Journey to Natural Form

'Our own physical body possesses a wisdom which we who inhabit the body lack. We give it orders which make no sense.'

—Henry Miller

We humans can learn from the animal world. Animals in their native environment often manage to stay in their natural physical form throughout their journey. It is so because they live in their homeland, typically a jungle environment. Now, look at us humans in a city environment. We encounter unnatural health issues in our constant chase and cannot escape the influence of fast and unhealthy foods, lifestyle disorders, and excessive work. It is not surprising to see these external influences corrupt our body's nature.

Don't we all wish to stay in our natural body form for as long as possible? This body state is achievable and begins with looking after our bodies comprehensively and consistently. We must look after our physical body to align with its natural biorhythm.

Let us delve into this concept of natural form in the context of our physical body. The natural body form is our ability to keep our body in its naturally gifted state without any excesses. Normally, excesses can be seen in the form of weight—over or under—or sleep- or stress-related issues that crop up on the visible body. Excesses can also provoke another set of issues in our internal bodies, leading to lifestyle or other chronic diseases. Whatever the case may be, your internal and external physical health will show through when you look at yourself in a state of stark nakedness.

Some people are born tall and lanky, while others have the gift of a broad frame or short structure. Your natural form is a combination of your natural skeletal frame and body composition just the way they were meant to be.

In the past, we were all fed with the narrative of how critical our genetic footprint was in determining our life's journey. However, research on Epigenetics has completely flipped that narrative. While we cannot alter our genetic predisposition, we can influence our gene expression based on the environment we subject ourselves to. Epigenetics—which focuses on the positive or negative genetic expression—allows us complete freedom to determine the qualitative outcomes of our genetic footprint.

The healthier and happier we keep our bodies, the healthier and happier the journey of our physical bodies. To head in the direction of true self-love, and eventually freedom, the health and wellness of our physical body is crucial. We need to love ourselves the way we were naturally made without worrying about the trends that might push us towards looking unnaturally fit or appealing. The aspiration must shift from the ego-fuelled body gods we see on glitzy magazine covers to staying in our nature-gifted body form and consistently looking after it. This state of being is guided by our inner wisdom, reflecting our true nature.

We need to understand and absorb this core philosophy that can elevate our journey of physical well-being and beyond. Programme your mind to focus on the fundamental call of the soul to be in its natural form. Look in the mirror to understand where you stand and resolve to return to your nature-gifted body. Remember to enjoy the journey of transition at every step of the way.

Physical Assessment: The Mirror Test

This is your moment of truth. Stand in front of a mirror—literally or metaphorically—with nothing on—yes, stark naked, just the way you were born. Now, thoroughly look at yourself and assess what you see with honesty. Observe every part of your body, externally and internally, with love, without negativity or judgement. Feel yourself conducting a detailed self-check and use the mirror as your magnifying glass that helps you take stock of your current reality. Look at the current state of your body and make a list of external and internal 'departures'. Some external departures can include hair loss, weak eyes, dark circles, premature ageing, untoned muscles, and excess or underweight conditions. On the other hand, internal issues can range from extreme weakness and lethargy to unexplainable pain in any part of the body to lifestyle disorders like hypertension, diabetes, PCOD, or gut issues. Internal issues that we are aware of as diagnosed medical issues are hopefully being dealt with already. If you feel other internal medical conditions are bubbling up and are being brushed under the carpet for reasons of fear, they need to be acknowledged and dealt with.

The key is to look at your body from the Soul Mind. Be the observer and talk to it to lay the truth bare. In being truthful, we will first acknowledge and then resolve to get back on track.

Below is a space where you can pen down your comprehensive list of internal and external departures, serving as a ready reckoner.

External/Visible Manifestations or Departures from Your Natural Form	**Internal Manifestations or Departures from Your Natural Form**

After listing all your departures, it is time for peaceful acceptance and a clear resolution to begin your journey towards recovery.

Renew You: A Scientific Perspective on the Reality of Transformation

For those who thought they were stuck with their lifestyle-related disorders for life, here is some good news. The science of transformation says that it takes seven days for your stomach lining to renew itself, 30 days for your skin, 90 days for your muscular-skeletal structure, and one year for your whole biological being to renew.

This proves that a complete transformation of your being down to practically every cell in your body is possible. Whether you want this change to be positive or negative is entirely yours.

As we focus on renewing the physical body in this section, we want to draw your attention to the six most vital aspects of physical well-being—movement, breath, nutrition, feel good; look even better, sleep—rest and recovery, and sex. We will introduce a solid general framework for you to follow. This framework has been put together by some of the best-known names in the wellness industry and entails a lot of experience. We will continue to encourage you to make intuitive adjustments based on how you feel.

MOVEMENT

Movement is the first step towards renewing our physical body and developing deeper self-love. The aim is to live a disease-free and joyful life. As we begin our journey towards a balanced movement routine, it is important to understand that the process is the hero, not the outcome. So, allow the process to culminate into the outcome and participate, wholeheartedly, in a composed state of being. Let your movements be a celebration and not a punishment. For those not accustomed to a regular movement routine, it may initially feel like excessive effort. However, you only need to stay consistent, and as you start to see the results—both in terms of how you feel and look—you will begin to enjoy the journey of transformation.

Movement should work towards maintaining a healthy heart and lungs, keeping you agile and flexible, building muscle strength and capacity to endure, and improving body coordination and balance. The ideal movement regimen could include yoga, strength, and cardiovascular training; however, the right measure would be best determined by your choice and suitability.

Routines can get monotonous, yet we will offer you a start-off kit that you can creatively change later with permutations and combinations of your choice. However, make sure you address all major body parts in the week.

A well-rested body is ready to take the onslaught of the day after the night's healing process. Thus, ideally, movement is best done in the morning as sunrise triggers serotonin, which offers one abundant energy to perform. If you work out in the evenings, we recommend keeping the intensity low to avoid straining your body and depleting your energy levels.

Before you start any movement routine, take a few moments to set your intention for the session. This should be a function of how well-rested you are and how hard you want to push yourself. Remember, let go of any draining thoughts at this moment and try to be present to soak in the direct benefits of your efforts.

The Natural Form Flow

The natural form flow has been carefully curated with the body's fundamental needs in mind. This will act as a comprehensive work plan to bring you back to your body's nature or its natural form.

This flow is based on the eight fundamentals of movement—strength, agility, endurance, flexibility, balance, mind-body coordination, cardiovascular health, and breath management.

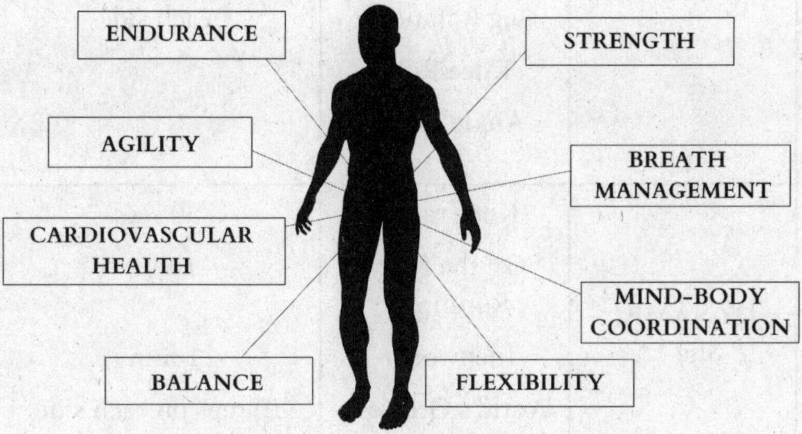

The Eight Fundamentals of Movement

This full-body flow includes compound exercises involving both dynamic and static movements. The sequence has been creatively curated to get you started on your movement journey, making you feel refreshed, energised, and deeply connected with yourself.

SECTION	MOVEMENT	RECOMMENDED REPETITIONS/TIME
WARM UP		
CIRCLES SET	Neck Rotations Wrist Rotations Shoulder Rolls Arm Rotations Hip Rotations Leg Rotations Knee Rols Ankle Rolls	5 rounds clockwise and anticlockwise on each side
DYNAMIC SET	Knee raises	30 secs
	On the Spot Running	1 min
	Inchworm	1 min
	World's Greatest Stretch	10 reps on each side
MAIN FLOW		
UPPER BODY	Overhead Spine Extension	10 deep breaths
	Forward Fold	5 reps followed by 10 deep breaths
	Side Bend	5 reps on each side, followed by 10 deep breaths on each side.

SECTION	MOVEMENT	RECOMMENDED REPETITIONS/TIME
SPINE AND CORE	Twist	5 reps on each side, followed by 10 deep breaths on each side
	Backward Bend	5 reps followed by 10 deep breaths
	Bird Dog	10 reps on each side
	Downward Dog to Upward Dog	10 reps
	Plank to Downward Dog with Toe Touches	45 secs
	Plank Hold	45 secs
	Mountain Climbers	45 secs
	Push-ups	10 reps x 3 sets
LOWER BODY	Deep Squat to Forward Fold	1 min
	Squats	10 reps x 3 sets
	Sumo Squats	10 reps x 3 sets
	Half Lunge and Hand Shuffle	10 reps each side x 2 sets

SECTION	MOVEMENT	RECOMMENDED REPETITIONS/TIME
COOL DOWN		
	Neck and Arm Release	1 min
	Wind Relieving Pose	30 secs on each side
	Figure Four Stretch	1 min on each side
	Happy Child's Pose	1 min
	Supine Twist	30 secs on each side
	Corpse Pose	2 mins +

You can access the natural form flow instructional video tutorial on our YouTube channel @sanyaasinthecity.

Natural Form Flow Guidelines

1. Complete each set of the flow with the recommended repetitions and hold for the recommended time.
2. Rest for 10–30 seconds between exercises. Rest more if you feel out of breath.
3. While 'natural form flow' is a comprehensive full-body movement plan, you may customise this

plan according to your requirements by increasing or reducing the intensity or repetitions of the movements targeting your trouble areas.

4. If you are nursing any injuries or sensitivities in the body, listen to your body and push yourself accordingly. If need be, you can adapt a movement to suit your comfort.
5. Hydration is important. Ensure that you are well-hydrated before and after the workout. We recommend sipping and not gulping water during the workout.
6. Wear comfortable, non-restrictive clothing that allows you to stretch in all directions during the practice.
7. You will require a yoga mat or rug for ease.
8. Practise in a well-ventilated room that's neither too hot nor too cold.
9. Follow this sequence 5–6 days a week and keep at least one day for rest and recovery.
10. Breath is paramount. A good oxygen supply is required to enable efficient movement. Synchronising your breath with movement also compounds the benefits of each exercise.
11. Be mindful of the target body part being worked upon for better engagement.
12. Ensure a minimum two-hour gap post your main meal and a minimum gap of 30–45 minutes post-snacking before you begin the natural form flow.

13. Complement the natural form flow with our recommended power ideas in 'nutrition', explained in detail in the next section of this toolkit.

With the help of natural form flow, you now have a solid starting point to get into the rhythm of a movement routine. While you can find several excuses to delay or distract yourself, we urge you to focus on the significant sanyaasi value of being self-focused, where the Soul Mind drives your motivation to move ahead, dispelling any distractions stemming from the ego or Body Mind. We must recognise that the physical body is the current home of the soul and needs to be taken care of just as we look after our homes.

BREATH

The science of yoga talks about the power of our breath in experiencing the interconnectedness between the body, mind, and source energy. Breath is one of the most vital aspects for conscious growth in the spirit world. Well-trained yoga experts emphasise the importance of breathwork every step of the way. All the learnt spiritual masters also train their disciples in meditation techniques, where breathwork is a crucial part of the practice.

Our first and last breath marks our time on earth. With our first breath, we begin our human journey, and with our last breath, we commence the process of leaving the human form. Such is the power and influence of breathing.

At the gross level, breath is the most vital, life-giving, and sustaining activity. At a subtle level, breath is the energiser of our life force called *prana*, responsible for keeping our entire inner network of *nadis* functioning optimally. The richer the quality of our breath, the more nourishment we provide to this network.

The only time we take notice of this life force is when we have trouble breathing, in the form of respiratory disorders. As life hits us during our formative years, so does stress. Before we know it, we become shallow breathers, trying to hit the finish line in a hurry. The vicious cycle of life-sucking stress depletes us of our most important life-sustaining activity—breathing. The slower we breathe, the longer and richer the quality of our life.

However, the pace of our breath and the pace of life create a chicken-and-egg situation. The question to be asked is whether pace leads to stress or if stress leads to pace. We get so lost in the grind that pace affects us both ways without us being aware of it. The eventual toll is unfortunately on the life-sustaining breath. The events of the day determine the pace of our breath, and in several instances, the pace of our breath determines the pace at which we operate. The common denominator in both situations is pace. It is almost as if the pace of our breath establishes the pace at which we grow. In this phase of reckless speed, we feel the high of life unfolding without realising the body's need to be calmer. We are subconsciously wired to connect the exhilaration of pace with the experience of a high, and consequently, with growth.

Most of us pay the least attention to our breathing. It tends to be unconscious and shallow, depriving the body of the required amount of oxygen for optimal health. In several instances, we inhale from the mouth, which is an unnatural way of breathing.

Irregular breathing disrupts brain rhythms, leading to physical, mental, and emotional energy blocks. This results in conflicts, restlessness, lack of mental clarity, lifestyle disorders, and diseases.

The slower we breathe, the more at peace we are. Self-love is synonymous with slow breathing, which is our fundamental nature. We can manage and maintain slow breathing initially by simply becoming conscious of our breath, particularly during moments of stress. Being aware of our breathing patterns will help us recognise the need and benefits of slowing down our breath in such times. As we progress on our self-love journey, our nature will ensure that we breathe slowly and easily. Our Soul Mind will naturally keep us grounded in slow breathing. The key is to spend as much time as possible in Soul Mind consciousness. By observing how our breath responds to stress, triggers, events, and disruptions, we can choose to redirect and reset our breathing patterns.

We must also be conscious of the quality of air we breathe as this has a direct bearing on how it works on our inner mechanisms. This commentary implies a connection between our inner and outer nature. Since we rely on the air we breathe from our external environment, we must be aware of our responsibility to keep it clean and pure. Given the global pollution issues we face, we must do our part to maintain a clean environment.

Your Guide to Breath for Health

In this toolkit, you will discover two vital methods to enhance the quality of your life by improving the nature of your breath. The first method is pranayama, the age-old yogic practice of breathwork on the pranic body, which will require you to set aside some dedicated time. These exercises are like a workout for fundamental correction of your inner body.

The second method is called round-the-clock breath consciousness, which involves being aware of your breath. Watching your breath throughout the day will help you observe how it changes based on the activities you perform, the people you meet, and the events that unfold. This awareness of your pace and rhythm of breathing will work as a natural alarm for you to get back to slow breathing.

Pranayama

Pranayama techniques activate and regulate the life force, enabling heightened awareness and energy within our bodies and minds. Therefore, pranayama is more than mere breathing exercises; it induces physical and mental well-being.

Below are exercises that, when performed consistently, will enhance your respiratory system's functioning. Pranayama helps establish rhythmic and slow breathing, reversing the negative effects of shallow breathing. A slow breathing rate keeps the heart strong, contributing to vitality and longevity.

1. **Kapalbhati** kriya is a purifying technique, a powerful practice for cleansing the frontal region of the brain the lungs, and the nasal passages. It helps purify the skull (*kapal*) and awaken one's spiritual energy, destroying the diseases afflicting the head. It strengthens the nervous system and tones the digestive organs.

   How to: Sit comfortably, with your spine straight on the floor or a chair. Take a few deep breaths. Exhale forcefully through your nose, pulling your belly towards your spine; the inhalation will be passive. Begin with a few rounds, increasing the duration and intensity as comfortable. Aim for two minutes initially. Practise on an empty stomach and before performing asanas.

2. **Bhastrika** helps awaken the Kundalini energy and purify the nadis. It is said to increase the digestive fire responsible for digestion, absorption, and elimination. The heat and energy produced during the practice increase vitality, overcoming lethargy.

   How to: Sit comfortably with your spine straight and your hands resting on the knees in gyan mudra (where the index finger is touching the thumb, while the other fingers are extended, and the palm is facing upwards).

   Close your eyes and take a few deep breaths to relax your body and mind.

   Begin by inhaling deeply through both nostrils, filling your lungs with air. Exhale forcefully through both nostrils, contracting the abdominal muscles.

   Immediately, inhale through both nostrils forcefully, fully expanding the abdominal muscles.

   Continue this rhythmic and rapid forceful inhalation and exhalation, without straining yourself. Coordinate the movement of your abdomen with your breath, expanding during inhalation and contracting during exhalation.

   Practise Bhastrika pranayama for a few rounds, gradually increasing the pace and duration as you become more comfortable. Beginners may start with 1–2 minutes and slowly extend to 5–10 minutes or more. After completing the practice, sit quietly for a few moments, observing its effects on the body and mind. Practise on an empty stomach, preferably in the morning, and avoid practising immediately after meals.

3. **Deep abdominal breathing** or diaphragmatic breathing is performed by enhancing the action of the diaphragm and reducing the action of the chest/ribcage. This is the most natural and efficient way to breathe to improve our physical and mental well-being. Properly using the diaphragm while breathing improves the circulation of oxygen in the blood, boosts cardiac functioning, and increases oxygen supply to the heart. It also reduces stress and allows us a deeper state of rest.

   How to: Sit comfortably with support or lie on your back. Keep one palm on your abdomen and another on your chest. Focus on your natural breathing for a few seconds before gradually deepening the inhalations and exhalations. Avoid straining your breath. With every breath in, push your abdomen out against your palm, and with every breath out, pull the belly towards the spine. Keep the movements gentle without straining the core. Focus on the inhalations, exhalations, and chest and abdomen movement. Continue for as long as you feel comfortable.

4. **Nadi shodhana pranayama** or alternate nostril breathing has calming effects, relieving anxiety and improving focus and concentration. Breathing through the left nostril tends to activate the right hemisphere of the brain and breathing through the right nostril activates the left-brain hemisphere. It is also known to balance the flow of breath in both nostrils, stabilising the energies within.

How to: Sit in a comfortable position and place your left palm in chin mudra (where the index finger is touching the thumb, while the other fingers are extended, and the palm is facing upwards) on the knee and your right palm in Vishnu mudra (curl the forefinger and middle finger in towards the palm of your hand). Close the right nostril with the right thumb. Inhale from the left nostril and for as long as you are comfortable. Close the left nostril with the last two fingers of the right hand and open the right nostril, exhaling comfortably. Lastly, inhale from the right nostril, close it, and exhale from the left nostril. This is one round. Practise for a minimum of 8–10 rounds.

5. **Bhramari pranayama** or the humming bee breath pranayama helps relieve stress and manage anger, anxiety, and insomnia. The practice also strengthens the vocal cords, improving the functioning and quality of voice. The humming sound creates a soothing and relaxing environment, relaxing the nervous system.

   How to: Place your thumbs in your ears, the first two fingers on your eyes, the third closer to the nostrils, and the little finger close to your mouth. Inhale deeply through both the nostrils and exhale while making a bee-like humming sound from the mouth. Practise this for 8 to 10 rounds.

Round-the-Clock Breath Consciousness

Slow breathing from our nostrils, and not the mouth, is key to a long and healthy life. We must make slow breathing the focal point in all our waking moments. While our natural breathing pattern slows down as we sleep, we must be conscious of our breathing while awake. For most of us, post the age of twelve, the normal breaths per minute can range from 12–20. We need to bring our number of breaths per minute closer or lower than twelve.

This slow and easy breath rate should only be altered when you are involved in intense physical activity, including workouts or cardiovascular training. We must also be conscious of not allowing our stressed mental state to dictate our breath rate. We are human and will naturally encounter stressful situations, however, our focus should be on regulating our breath during these moments.

Simple awareness of one's natural breathing is enough to deepen and slow down the rate of respiration, leading to a more relaxed rhythm.

Note: For readers who wish to follow along with these breathwork techniques, detailed instructional videos are available on our YouTube channel: @sanyaasinthecity.

Nutrition

We are what we eat. Thousands of years ago, when we were hunter-gatherers, nature made us choose what we ate. The only determinant for people's choices was instinct, intuition, and what was naturally available. Life was simple yet fulfilling. When we became agriculturists, we experienced changes in our lifestyles as we moved less and ate what we grew. Along the way, we did everything possible to take us away from intuitive natural eating.

Nutrition plays a vital role in our quest for self-love. Somewhere in our hectic lives, we have lost the significance of feeding our bodies with the responsibility of looking after them. We feed our bodies all the wrong foods, in disproportionate quantities, and at the wrong hours, expecting our bodies to function optimally. Moreover, modern cities have enabled easy access to foods from all parts of the world, which might be appropriate for locals from that part of the world but completely inappropriate for the environment you live in.

Our ancestors would gather to celebrate their meals, savouring the taste with gratitude, awareness, and love. The food was freshly sourced and made with love and patience. Efforts were made to source quality ingredients and hours were spent preparing a dish to perfection. The demands of urban living today have forced us to abandon this age-old approach to eating. Today, we eat hurriedly and on the go. We also struggle to set aside time to source good quality ingredients for our meals. Additionally, what we eat is probably made with equal haste and lacks the secret sauce of love.

The constant bombardment of fad diets and new eating patterns promise to get us into shape. Stories of celebrities achieving amazing results using these methods tempt us to try them, too. However, we often hear about people quickly regaining the weight they lost or the failure of certain magical diets to produce results. We also hear of deficiencies or deeper health complications due to these fads. The solution is to approach this vital aspect of nutrition from the viewpoint of simplicity and innate intelligence, which will point us towards eating fresh and local food. Our intelligence naturally guides us to consume more fresh fruits and vegetables for the body's smooth functioning, along with food cooked with love. Here, love takes centre stage yet again.

Do not wait for a medical incident to make amends to your diet. As it is said, prevention is better than cure, it is a lot smarter to proactively chart your course towards nourishing your body. Most importantly, understand where you went wrong and set clear goals for staying true to your natural self. Our constant endeavour is to guide you back to nature, no matter how far you have strayed.

Due to the never-ending and contradictory opinions on nutrition, it is easy to get confused. Keeping this in mind, we have assembled a set of power tools you can implement, which serve as easy markers to filter your choices of what, when, and how much food you must consume for your body's optimum functioning. These tools start with applying your intuitive power to decide what goes on your plate, which we call the 'art of intelligent eating'. This is followed by the second power tool, the 'base theory', which outlines a simple yet supremely effective flow in eating that can be applied to all your meals. The final tool is called the 'positive thought ecosystem', which has the potential to work wonders when applied with the right mindset while eating.

Power Tool #1: The Art of Intelligent Eating

The best nutritionists and pharmacists lie within our intuitive mind. This way of Soul Mind thinking discerns the appropriate nutritional needs of the body and calls upon its natural pharmacy from within to deal with challenges. Some conscious individuals prioritise themselves, staying in their natural form. For most of us, however, life creates a dent, which can look like extreme weight gain or loss, diseases, or other lifestyle-related issues.

In our quest to get back, while it is a great idea to follow the practical advice of professionals, we should also be self-aware and listen to our body's intelligence and instinct. This leads us towards exploring this interesting and profound world of self-knowingness as the best guide.

The art of intelligent eating enables us to create our unique nutrition plan based on our body's intelligence. This intelligence makes us think about the food we plan to eat in addition to making us mindful of the consequences of what we have chosen. It also makes us aware of the entire equation, starting with what and how much we choose to eat to how our choices impact our gut health, including digestion and excretion. In this approach, the gut decides what we consume instead of our mouth, senses, and desires. This is an intuitive guide to creating food menus based on what our body craves to keep it in its natural form.

When we tune into our inner intelligence, we make nature-aligned choices. We also become more conscious about our eating and drinking habits. However, do not mistake this as an approach to eating boring or staid food; we can remain foodies and eat the foods we have always craved. The difference is in creating a better balance by mindfully choosing ingredients and cooking methods and managing cheat meals with intelligence.

Whether you are a foodie or a functional food eater, your choices will naturally align in the right direction. This approach does not have any dos or don'ts, nor are there any good or bad foods. Feel free to be a vegetarian or a meat-eater, whatever works for you. The secret is in maintaining balance.

Power Tool #2: The Base Theory

This concept involves a set pattern of eating throughout the day to enhance nourishment, easy digestion, and efficient excretion. Use this method as a simple reference to help you navigate the complex world of choices.

The core idea of this theory is to start each main meal by creating a base of fruits or vegetables. This base allows you to eat whatever you want for your main meal, including meats or other indulgent foods. This approach will help aid digestion and excretion by forming an easy pathway.

Consume your base foods about half an hour before your meal, ensuring the portion is substantial.

The secret to nutrition lies in mindfully eating what you enjoy, making digestion, absorption, and excretion effortless. We all desire to finish each meal feeling light and to wake up with a clean digestive system. Once accustomed to this, it becomes essential for peace and happiness, as your gut starts to influence your dietary choices.

If you establish a proper base, you will resolve most of your nutrition and nourishment-related issues at the source.

The Base Foods We Recommend

Breakfast: Start your morning with fresh or dried fruits, depending on what your system can handle, as the base of your breakfast. Ensure a 30-minute gap between your base and the main breakfast.

Alternatively, you can have vegetable juice. Include vegetables like carrots, beetroot, spinach, celery, kale, ginger, fresh turmeric, and mint leaves. You may also add fruits like green apples or gooseberries to your vegetable juice if desired.

Lunch: Consume a fair-sized bowl of raw or cooked vegetable salad about half an hour before lunch. The natural roughage from the vegetable base will help cleanse, regulate, and fortify the digestive system. Once you have your base, you can handle a regular main meal of any vegetarian or non-vegetarian option. Even if you overindulge in your main course, your system will manage digestion and excretion effectively.

Dinner: Cooked vegetables, whether stir-fried, steamed, boiled, or grilled, are ideal for your dinner base. Another option is vegetable soup, consumed about half an hour before your main meal. Try to have dinner as early in the evening as possible and keep it light. The vegetable base will aid in digestion and excretion.

Power Tool #3: The Positive Thought Ecosystem

Many of us carry our troubles with us when we sit down to eat—whether it's rushing to tackle the next task or being stressed about work, illness, or any other mind-bending issue. As a result, we end up swallowing the food, without even chewing properly.

This backdrop of how we feel at the time we choose to eat has a massive bearing on how that food works for us. We may think we have done well by eating a nutritious meal but if consumed in a hurry and with a worry, the meal ingested becomes toxic and non-absorbent.

Simply put, the thought energy generated while eating can be positive or negative. Negative thoughts will lead to a toxic chemical cocktail mixing with our blood, spreading negativity to every cell in our body. Even the nutritional value of the most wholesome meal becomes vitiated in a negative environment. Conversely, positive thinking while eating enhances the positive effect of food on our bodies. Even a less nutritious meal can do wonders in a positive thought environment.

Despite whatever is going on in your life, make conscious eating a priority, building a positive connection with your food. Make eating and drinking activities you look forward to. You will soon notice a substantial difference between eating to get by and eating to savour your meals, automatically moving from gulping down your food to thoroughly enjoying the process.

Positive feelings of love, thankfulness, nourishment, and healing must be attached to the food we consume. This simple yet effective shift in thinking can have a massive impact on how the food we eat can nourish and heal our bodies from within.

Handy Cues for Nutrition Management

Below are some steps that will help you build intelligence and improve the biofeedback of your body:

1. Inculcate a virtuous habit of eating slowly, as it helps focus on the taste, aroma, colour, and texture of the meal, improving the absorption of nutrition.
2. Eating slowly will help you chew your food properly, aiding in the primary digestion that begins in the buccal cavity.

3. Sit comfortably with a straight spine as it ensures the proper movement of food inside the body, enhancing the digestion and absorption processes. Avoid squeezing or bending your abdomen while eating.
4. Always wash your hands thoroughly before every meal. Eat with your fingers if possible as the sense of touch adds a sensory connection of feeling your food, thus, enhancing your intimacy with it.
5. Your meals should ideally be from pan to plate as freshly cooked meals enhance their nutritive value.
6. Ensure that all the ingredients used for cooking are as natural as possible. The fruits and vegetables should be fresh, local, seasonal, and regional.
7. Do not underestimate the power of consuming food cooked with love and care. There must be intimacy in making, serving and eating food.
8. Eat when you are hungry, ideally, once you have digested your previous meal. Follow the 80/20 principle to your meal plans: Eat only up to 80 per cent of your hunger capacity. This principle can also be applied to how you balance your cheat meals. Ensure you consume healthy and nourishing meals 80 per cent of the time and restrict your cheat meals to not more than 20 per cent.
9. Maintain a food journal if you want a deeper understanding of your gut's processing power regarding intolerances and allergies.
10. Your dinner should be submaximal, with a gap of 2–3 hours before sleeping for proper digestion.

11. The food you consume subconsciously influences the way you feel. Consuming more prana and energy-giving foods, such as a balanced vegetarian diet rich in fruits, vegetables, lentils, nuts, and seeds, is believed to make you feel light and energetic, assisting the quest to grow spiritually. As you evolve in your self-love journey, you will naturally start making conscious food decisions.
12. If your intake of animal protein is high, follow the base theory religiously to balance your nourishment with essential fibre, antioxidants, vitamins, and minerals.
13. If you have any vices, which most of us do in a typical city environment, plan to add effective antidotes to neutralise their harmful effects. For instance, if you like a drink or two regularly, add alkaline foods like beetroot, gooseberry, pomegranate, milk thistle, and fresh lemon juice to your antidote plan. This will neutralise the acidosis and inflammation caused by alcohol.
14. We would never recommend and advise smoking to anyone, however, if you are struggling to wean it down or kick the habit, we suggest you include antioxidants such as vitamins C and E through a healthy dose of fresh fruits and vegetables to reverse the cell damage. Between two puffs, take at least four to five deep breaths, as if you are blowing up a balloon. Each time you take a puff, you burn two air sacs in your lungs, so this oxygen stimulation provides some relief to your lungs.

FEEL GOOD, LOOK EVEN BETTER

We reflect our inner world in the way we look. If we are clean, loving, and beautiful on the inside, we shine the same state of being in our outer representation. Deeper in the journey of self-love, we will naturally lean towards making sustainable, eco-friendly, and eco-conserving choices in our grooming routines. On the other side of the spectrum, we cross paths with individuals who appear scruffy, reflecting their inner chaos. We do come across cases where people struggling with their inner distress either neglect or lack the motivation and confidence to prioritise personal grooming.

As we work on building movement and managing our nutrition in our daily routines, we must also pay equal attention to how we look after grooming and present ourselves to the world. Have you ever worn bright colours on a gloomy day and felt an immediate surge of positivity? Have you tried to dress sharply with clean and well-ironed clothes to feel a spring in your step? Personal care must be integral to our daily self-love practice to enhance our journey towards inner connectedness. This habit, often unconsciously, has a positive and uplifting effect on our day. Feeling and looking good is a vital part of this comprehensive approach.

The idyllic seaside town of Cannes in the South of France is famous for its glitzy film and media festivals. However, there is a different dimension to the Cannes culture you might not know. For the most part, Cannes is a sleepy town with a largely ageing population. The average age is about 50 years. If you travel to Cannes during the off-season, you will notice that the local population is impeccably dressed. They look so good that they exude a sense of being in love with themselves.

This phenomenon in Cannes is almost infectious. One thing is for sure—you will not feel good if you walk the streets of Cannes looking scruffy!

Personal grooming is an important aspect of looking and feeling good on our journey to absolute self-love. It is important to *be* and *feel* clean, ensuring basic hygiene on all fronts. Do not mistake grooming and dressing well for an opulent wardrobe. Nor are we talking about accumulating excessive clothes and products to feel good. We must groom and dress in a way that enhances our persona, reflecting inner joy and vibrancy. Brands and badges do not matter.

Often, people on a material chase dress to please or compete with others. They love to show their wealth or status through expensive brands and accessories. This, then, moves towards a race to conquer, where people want to outdo others. This is a trap brimming with frustrations and draining energy.

The goal is to dress in a way that enhances your persona while maintaining simplicity at its core. As you expand on the ethos of simple yet effective personal grooming, you may be drawn to interesting directions. For some, this might imply an uncomplicated, functional, and minimal style, such as a simple tee and jeans; for others, sustainability might be a key factor. It could be a combination of these elements or something else altogether. The trick is to keep it joyous, using it as a means of self-expression. As you delve deeper into self-care and self-love, you will find that feeling good from within makes you look better, and striving to look good can improve how you feel. This synergy of feeling good on the inside and being attentive towards your outer appearance contributes to your *aakarshan*.

SLEEP: REST AND RECOVERY

Duality rules the roost in the world we live in. Where there is day, there is night. Where there is work, there is also this bodily need to rest. Life oscillates from activity to passivity. As much as activity is important, so is passivity. If you haven't done enough justice to the activity, your passivity—or the resting part—will suffer. However, if you do not get adequate rest, it will be difficult to function optimally.

Sleep is the most critical part of rest and recovery. This is when our body and mind recover from the vagaries of a hectic day and its impact on us. While we are aware of the significance of sleep, we use it as the most easily negotiable part of our day—we compromise sleep at the drop of a hat.

We all remember our school and college days, when sleeping less was a way of life. Most of the intensive studies took place at night, accompanied by numerous cups of coffee. In these early years, the lack of adequate sleep did not bother us much. For many of us, this habit continues into the middle years of our lives, where it starts to manifest into bigger problems.

Talk to most middle-aged individuals and you may hear stories of sleep deprivation being a part of their lifestyles. You may also come across stories of high achievers claiming they hardly need any sleep. However, if you talk to them a few years later, you are likely to hear about their health issues.

Sleep, much like movement and nutrition, is vital to staying true to our natural form. We must prioritise guarding our time for rest and recovery. We should shift from viewing sleep as something easily sacrificed to making it a priority. Our ultimate goal is to sleep like a baby and wake up feeling refreshed. The appropriate amount of sleep depends on two distinct factors—the duration of sleep and the quality of sleep.

The Quantitative Aspect of Sleep

Human beings are made with a macro design that works for most. Part of the design is to rest and recover after a hard day's work. Typically, we need between 7–8 hours of restful sleep to stay healthy. Just as we intentionally charge our phones every day to keep them from losing power, we must consciously charge our bodies with adequate sleep to keep them from running out of power.

Any departure from the systematic need to sleep enough often leads to incidents or accidents. Why do we get caught up in staying up for longer hours in a day than our bodies can naturally handle? The impact of the collective noise field convinces us to live this unnatural life. Most of us run hectic schedules in an urban environment and want our days to extend into late nights. We believe ourselves to be superhumans, capable of leading this lifestyle forever. While we understand the demands of an action-packed city day, it is crucial to manage our activities to ensure time for rest and recovery.

Power Thought: 'I will make time to rest come what may.'

Just like you eat at regular intervals, you need to prioritise the duration of your sleep. If you bring the concept of intuitive living into the dimension of rest and recovery, you will find yourself listening to your body's need to rest adequately.

The Qualitative Aspect of Sleep

Sleep disorders have managed to hit epidemic proportions. The number of people who make adequate time to rest and recover yet complain about not being able to sleep well is massive. We want to ideally hit the sack and be able to sleep within a few minutes. However, it is but a dream for most of us.

Why does our natural sleep quality take a hit in a typical urban ecosystem? Why does this material chase take its toll on mental health?

When we take a moment to introspect, we look at the web we have fallen into. Most of us carry the load of the day's events into the night as we have more time to ourselves in the evenings. Positive or negative fluctuations during the day can significantly impact our natural biorhythms, robbing us of our inner peace and affecting the quality of our rest and recovery.

Additionally, people spend more time consuming content across media platforms, particularly during the evening. One can safely presume that most of the content contains violence and unsavoury themes. Negative-themed content can also adversely affect the nature and quality of our resting time.

The first thing you need for a restful sleep is peace of mind. The challenges of the day must be dealt with deftly and comprehensively during the day itself. Once the sun sets, the goal should be to start unwinding from these stresses and move towards neutralising their toll on us. The art of letting go can be cultivated with a little practice. Letting go can become more natural by finding a peace stimulant that works for you and absorbing the peace from it. Train your mind to be spontaneous in the moment without the baggage of the past day or the worry of the impending night.

A walk in nature-rich surroundings, focusing on absorbing it with all your senses, is a good way to ease into the evening. You could also try sound-based meditation with nature sounds to feel at peace. These are just some examples of peace stimulants that can help you feel light and relaxed before going to bed. Feel free to be guided by your intuitive suggestions to find your peace stimulants.

Realistically, there will be days when unpleasant situations cause sleep disruptions. On such days, don't try to fight the overwhelming feeling of sleeplessness. Understand that this is a phase and will pass naturally.

The Practical Toolkit for Restful Sleep

1. Avoid getting into excitable mind states a few hours before you sleep.
2. Ensure adequate movement throughout the day.
3. Ensure proper nutrition in all the meals throughout the day, eating consciously and in balance. Avoid overeating and heavy meals, especially at night, to sleep comfortably.
4. An orgasm can have a relaxing effect on the body, as it acts like a natural sleeping pill.
5. If you suffer from chronic sleep issues, try yoga nidra around your sleep time.
6. Avoid exposure to any gadget (TV, mobile, etc.) at least 30 minutes before you sleep.
7. Natural remedies like ashwagandha, chamomile tea, and turmeric milk are effective sleep enablers.
8. Avoid wearing tight clothes while sleeping. If possible, sleep naked or opt for loose and breathable fabrics.
9. Soak your feet in warm water and massage hot oil or clarified butter (ghee) on the soles of your feet before sleeping.

10. Try to sleep on your left side as it improves blood circulation and helps you breathe better.
11. Use a slim pillow for better spinal alignment, aiding in restful sleep.
12. Follow this simple yoga sequence to improve your sleep quality and quantity or do it along with our instructional video on our YouTube channel: @sanyaasinthecity:
    - Vajrasana (thunderbolt pose)
    - Balasana (child's pose)
    - Marjariasana and Bitilasana (cat and cow pose)
    - Paschimottanasana (seated forward fold)
    - Viparita karani asana (legs up the wall)
    - Baddha Konasana (butterfly pose)
    - Bhramari pranayama (humming bee breathing)
    - Nadi shodhana pranayama (alternate nostril breathing)
    - Shavasana (corpse pose)

Other Aspects of Rest and Recovery

a. Get a massage every week to help the recovery of your strained muscles. You can also invest in a shiatsu massager that can be used every day at home.

b. Round-the-clock-breath consciousness is another great tool to keep your mind at peace throughout the day.

c. A power nap during the day can keep you adequately rested throughout the day.

d. Make time for your loved ones regularly. These interactions unconsciously help you stay centred and relaxed.

e. Spend time in nature as it is extremely healing. Make a conscious connection with nature each day as it helps release the happy hormones.

f. Cuddle often as it is a power tool that aids the feel-good factor.

g. Allocate time to pursue intrinsic interests like reading, writing, or playing an instrument or sport.

h. Don't take yourself too seriously and make time to be childlike and playful.

i. Incorporate a daily meditation for your holistic health. Create a meditation flow that can tap into different meditative practices like chanting, breath focus, and visualisation.

SEX

Sex as a subject is of the highest interest to humans. The clear reason for this sex appeal is that it leads us to the ultimate pleasure we experience in the human form—the amazing 'O'.

While sex is one of the most natural experiences for humans, it is still a matter of taboo or is not spoken about openly in several cultures. In reality, sex is the purest form of energy exchange between two individuals. It is crucial to understand that, at its core, sex is nature. It is the truth behind evolution—from humans to animals and beyond. The reality of sex is divine, given the beauty and pleasure of the act and its potential outcome.

The paradoxical nature of sex brews in our minds in our early years, sparking intrigue due to the secretive atmosphere surrounding the topic.

In our early years, many of us explore our intimate, pleasure-giving body parts and areas. A little playing around with ourselves feels good, which leads to an inner yearning to explore further. As we grow up and the cautionary noise around the topic intensifies, we invariably start associating a sense of shame and guilt with sex. For a lot of us, this rhetoric on the subject at home and in our interactions often drowns our sense of pleasure associated with the reality of our sexual experiences. The outer conditioning on the subject contradicts our inner yearning to explore our bodies. We can get confused about the beautiful reality of sex, which stunts our sexual experiences, in this paradox of the inner experience and outer noise.

Despite the confusion of the early years, the overpowering blissful experience of our first orgasm makes having sex and thinking about it a comfortable and pleasurable corner for most. It becomes such a powerful aspect of our formative years that the manifestations range from being obsessed with sex to becoming a vital part of our existence. Very few escape the overwhelming power of sex in the early to mid-years.

At the material end of the spectrum, a large majority of individuals experience sex as a functional need of the body and go through it routinely. There is a method to this madness. This templated act of sex is motivated by our own selfish desires for pleasure with little to no care for our partner's needs.

The other extreme of the spectrum comes with pure love at the source of divine lovemaking. This side of the spectrum opens our minds to the true potential of sex. This is the free end of the spectrum where lust, conditioning, personal insecurities, or societal norms do not influence our experiences. This is a world of love and freeness where sex is divine, motivated by this burning desire to pleasure the partner and the orgasms experienced are far more earth-shattering compared to anything a person might have ever experienced. These peak orgasms open the doorway to the yearning to aim for higher states of consciousness where the bliss quotient is even higher.

In the context of the two sides of the spectrum, it is important to understand this journey of experiencing an orgasm from a base level to its highest potential, the peak orgasm.

Power Tool: Journey from the Small O to the Peak O

It is a universal truth that the O in our lives is the best feeling we encounter in our body form. How many of us have experienced the varying intensities of this O? For most individuals, this is neither a thought that has consciously occurred nor a reality that has sunk in. At the most material level of having meaningless sex sits the shallow field of the regular O, while the most powerful orgasms can be experienced in meditative lovemaking. It is important to take a few minutes to introspect your experiences thus far. Whatever the case, the very premise that the intensity of our experience can be enhanced manifold will be an exciting prospect for all. The joy of the O can be enhanced to unbelievable levels by understanding the simplicity of the process.

We believe in consistently showing you the journey back to your nature. When we are on a path of self-love, we move from expecting and transacting to being loved and emanating love in all our actions. This is what happens in our act of lovemaking as well. We encounter a meditative feeling of wanting to give more without expectations. We transition from being selfish in bed to being selfless and prioritise our partner's happiness and satisfaction. It is in this act of giving that we experience the highest states of pleasure ourselves. The beauty of this karma lies in the subconscious change in our partner's behaviour; thus, enhancing the overall experience for both individuals. Such is the miraculous nature of being selfless.

Being in the act with our Soul Mind—with all our bodily senses immersed—takes us on a meditative journey that is glass-shattering or an O to the power of many.

Issues like performance anxiety that people have around lovemaking naturally resolve, leading us to this ultimate orgasmic feeling called the peak O. It is in this state that we recognise the shallowness of all the material sex and the Os we have experienced in the past. In this state of the peak O, bliss is felt by the entire body and beyond. It must be experienced to be understood.

At this point, we encounter a feeling of timelessness, spacelessness, and nothingness. The process and the outcome become meditative and blissful. This is the first real experience of transcendence, and for many individuals, it is the start of a deeper exploration of this blissful state.

Toolkit to Enhance Sexual Experience

1. **Being in Love with Yourself:** When your love for yourself is on the higher side, you naturally express it in all outward manifestations. Sex is at the forefront of where it will show through, making the experience more meaningful and satisfying. Once you are done reading this book in its totality, the myriad tools shared to increase your love hub on the physical, mental, and spiritual levels will act as enablers in your self-love journey.
2. **Freeness:** Sex needs to be experienced in free space, without the baggage of good, bad, or ugly as markers. Releasing all expectations from yourself and your partner can set you free. It is in the freeness of possibilities that experiments and new highs occur.
3. **Love Is the Ultimate Truth:** As humans, we are naturally attracted to people. We can be attracted to multiple people throughout our lives. As long as love is the source of your relationships, sex can be a beautiful expression of that love.
4. **There Is Nothing Like the Perfect Sexual Experience:** Don't we all feel under pressure with the thought of having this perfect sexual experience? In today's ecosystem, besides the general banter on the topic, there is a whole world of perception-building that happens through the medium of porn. This world creates performance benchmarks for us, making us feel our experience is suboptimal. The truth of experiencing sex is to let it unfold intuitively.

5. **Be Egoless:** There is no room for ego to get in the way of purity. Ego may hold you back from completely expressing yourself without inhibitions and with intimacy.
6. **Be Naturally Curious:** The miracle of lovemaking is that no two experiences need to be the same. The moment we attach our instinct of curiosity to the act, we find ourselves exploring new experiences on each occasion. This curiosity leads to keeping boredom and dullness away from the bedroom. This curiosity also fosters creativity that can be explored in multiple ways. Be free to let your intuition guide you.
7. **Communicate:** Most of us come hardwired with a programme of minimal communication when it comes to the topic of sex. We carry on suffering suboptimal experiences yet are shy to talk about it with our partners. In love, the first principle is to open lines of communication on all possible topics, most importantly sex. This openness of communication can help us reach new heights.
8. **The Power of Your Natural Fragrance:** When we love ourselves, we tend to be clean both inside and outside. We have a natural fragrance that smells better than any fragrance one could buy from the top brands. The best mood setter is the natural fragrance of the genitalia, which can be an instant turn-on for both partners. In a love-fuelled relationship, this natural fragrance becomes the most intoxicating aphrodisiac to get us in the mood.

9. **Timing:** There is no right or wrong time to make love with your partner. The only truth here is being able to live intuitively and listen to your instincts that make you want it. Such is the power of truth. If the feeling is overwhelming and natural, chances are your partner will respond favourably at any time of the night or day.

10. **Being Meditative:** Lovemaking should be experienced with purity and complete involvement of all the senses. In the state of nothingness, we lose track of all our worries and troubles, helping us lose inhibitions regarding ourselves or our partner. This is a state of pure being and giving. If you find yourself struggling with being present, all you need to do is focus on making it a divine experience for your partner.

11. **The Karmic Rebound:** The beauty of being meditative and giving during lovemaking profoundly impacts your partner's response. The purity of intent provokes an unspoken yet equally enlightened response from your partner. This experience teaches that the best way to receive is not to expect, but to give.

12. **In the Absence of a Partner:** Nature has engineered us to find sexual gratification on our own. Masturbation is a natural and normal way to be sexually satisfied without a partner. There is nothing wrong with self-gratification. It is perfectly normal and can be used whenever you feel the need.

The physical body is the chariot of the Soul Mind. In loving and nourishing it, we are essentially caring for its current abode. It is crucial to work on the physical body in its entirety to align with our true self. All aspects of physical health—movement, nutrition, sleep, personal grooming, and sex—need to be assessed for deviations. Additionally, fundamental corrections need to be made wherever required. A balanced and healthy physical body is a step closer to living in freeness and operating from the Soul Mind.

6.2

Mental Body: The Journey from Body Mind to Soul Mind

'A sound mind in a sound body is a short but full description of a happy state in this world.'

—John Locke

We all understand the supreme power of our minds. The way we think determines a large part of our journeys, making it essential to keep this CPU healthy. A virtuous mind would typically be tuned more to listen to the heart—it needs to be driven by our love selves. We are used to the mind being the centre of logic in the ways we process information and act on it. The direction we are suggesting may seem like an antithesis to the common understanding of the use of our minds, however, therein lies the simple yet monumental clincher.

The conditioning of our early years is so firmly grounded in the equation of the mind being equal to logic that we cannot imagine a paradigm where we completely change the logic of the mind from rationality to heartfulness. It is in this flipped logic that we open the doors to transforming confusion into mind control and clarity. This new paradigm clears our minds to understand the myriad emotions we experience in an observing capacity and their best management for spiritual growth. We transition from being overly analytical and logical to becoming more emotionally attuned and compassionate.

A mind driven by love would be in tune with our Soul Mind. This mind state would lead us towards natural mind control and clarity while helping us navigate our actions, emotions, and relationships with greater dexterity.

Let us delve into each facet to better understand this hypothesis.

MIND CONTROL

The earlier we take charge of our mental faculties, the happier our journeys will be. Can we prevail over our thoughts, emotions, and physical manifestations in our bodies? The answer is an emphatic yes!

Often, we look at our body and mind as separate entities, when, in reality, they are deeply interconnected. Our mind is the hotbed for most of what we experience in the physical form. Whatever the state of our physical body today, it is a function of how kind or unkind our mind has been in its innate thinking. The truth, therefore, is that we script our stories in our minds.

It is important to understand that the mind in our physical body does not necessarily sit in our brain. Our body comprises trillions of thinking cells, making our whole physical form an interconnected thinking form. This interconnected thinking form, for most individuals, is conditioned to believe that the physical body is subject to mortality, corruptibility, and affectability. We have been referring to this perspective as the Body Mind.

In our human experience, we are conditioned to think with our Body Mind, responsible for creating our self-image, popularly called the 'I' image or the ego. Moreover, it is also the CPU of all our thoughts and feelings. This state of thinking is vulnerable to being deeply affected by events and situations. The problem with using the Body Mind faculty is that we get trapped and attached to the 'I', which is the limited comprehension of our real selves, which—based on name, position, fame, and material—is our world as comprehended by the mind of our physical body.

In our day-to-day living, we experience the good, the bad, and the ugly in cycles. If we allow the highs or the lows of an event to affect us regularly, we become vulnerable to being affected at our core, resulting in real damages. It's important to feel that high of a promotion or the low of losing a loved one; however, we need to quickly bounce back to our natural state. The power tool here is to make a subtle shift in thinking from our Body Mind to our Soul Mind.

Our soul cannot be affected by the vagaries of our physical body. We need to invoke our thinking ability from the mind of our soul. We have been referring to this as the Soul Mind, which operates from a state of knowledge that we are beyond the physical body. The soul is immortal, incorruptible, and unaffectable. Suddenly, all our worries and problems related to any aspect of our lives or death seem trivial and manageable. We witness life situations from the Soul Mind awareness, recognising that all is transient, and we are much bigger than ourselves, our thoughts, and our emotions. We accept whatever comes our way with trust and an inner belief that everything happens for a reason. Once we begin living from our Soul Mind, each experience strengthens our ability to think from our Soul Mind. This leads to a stiller state of being—as if we have a permanent meditative mind state.

Invoking our Soul Mind thinking helps us understand that what we are going through is to be witnessed without overattachment. It is akin to watching ourselves act in a film of our life story without getting affected by the twists and turns of the plot. This feeling of simply being is usually experienced in meditation. The application of Soul Mind makes our life experiences peaceful.

For further clarity on how the two mind states can potentially respond to an event, look at the table on the next page where a person has landed a job as the CEO of their dream company.

The next logical step is to look within and perform a self-assessment of your current state of mind. Below is a short list of questions that can help you understand the mindset you are operating from in any situation.

- Am I getting positively or negatively overaffected by what I am going through?
- Is what I'm going through emotionally lasting for too long?
- Once I put in the effort, do I get overly attached to the outcome?

If your answers are 'yes' to most of these questions, you are using the Body Mind.

If the answers to most of the questions below are 'yes' as well, you are heading towards Soul Mind thinking:

Body Mind State	Soul Mind State
Elation and a sense of achievement that accompanies validation and acceptance from society.	Witness the event and feel good about the achievement without creating an imbalance in the mind.
Experience a heightened ego boost, which, if unchecked, can lead the individual to function and act from the ego state.	Revert to one's natural state quickly, where the individual functions and acts from the love state.
Greed, selfishness, control, domination, delusions of grandeur, and personal power can act as the drivers of leadership.	Selflessness, compassion, empathy, value creation, and a collaborative spirit are the leadership traits.
Navigate this new ship either from overconfidence or from a fearful space.	Navigate this new ship from a state of intuitive flow and free space.

- Can I watch the events of my life—positive or negative—without feeling their impact for long?
- Am I able to break the never-ending cycle of desires leading to mindless material expectations?
- Do I believe in the immortality and nucleus of pure love of the soul?

The key is to shift the mind from your material brain to the free soul. This can seem a tad theoretical at this stage, however, absolute belief in the presence of a soul can help you internalise this new way of thinking.

Here is a visualisation technique that can help you transcend the Body Mind and tap into the potential of the Soul Mind:

> Imagine your awareness, like a halo, shifting slightly over your head. Picture this as being the mind of your beautiful and loving soul. Now apply the principles of how the soul would think and respond to the situation.

The illustration on the next page shows how wisdom is passed on from the Soul Mind to the Body Mind in challenging situations. The Body Mind receives and embraces this wisdom as it sees the practicality and virtuosity of this approach, acting almost instantly. Repeatedly affirm these nuggets of wisdom to align your Body Mind with the Soul Mind.

This is a great way to experience this magical state of thinking from the Soul Mind. This state might not come naturally in the initial stages, however, be patient till you eventually get there. It is a knack that can be cracked with consistent practise.

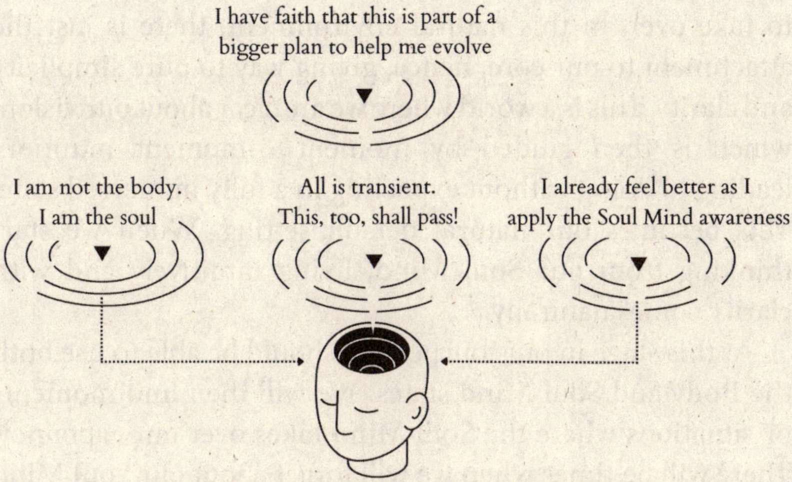

The Soul Mind Conditioners

MIND CLARITY

Our Body Mind thrives in the confines of the material world fuelled by logic, science, and the unending chase. The capacity of our Body Mind is marginal compared to the quantum capacity of our Soul Mind. We can attribute our lack of clarity in critical life situations to the limited nature of the Body Mind. The more we act from the Body Mind, the more we distance ourselves from our truth. It is then only natural to find ourselves drowned in chaos, fear, suffering, and confusion.

The danger of becoming enslaved by the lure of our desires is a potent by-product of being a Body Mind thinker. The yearning for our desires, coupled with our overattachment to their fulfilment, can create immense dissonance within us.

The moment we are clear about loving ourselves and chart our journeys in that direction, we witness our nature starting to take over. In this natural environment, there is just the attachment to our core, hence, giving way to pure simplicity and clarity. This is a world where we are clear about our vision, which is then guided by moment-to-moment intuition, leading to doing without expecting in a fully immersed state. This becomes our natural default setting. When we start thinking from our Soul Mind, living intuitively and with clarity comes naturally.

At this stage in our journey, we should be able to use both the Body and Soul Mind states. We will then find moments or situations where the Soul Mind takes over our captaincy. There will be times when we will forget about our Soul Mind and act from our Body Mind. We should now be able to witness the potential chaos emanating from the use of our Body Mind and see the tremendous value of Soul Mind awareness and application.

The Soul Mind operates in a field of pure potentiality and absolute creativity. This is a world where there is no space, time, or limitation of science and logic. At the level of your soul, you have the freedom and the creative skills to follow your nature. There is crystal clarity at every step. Moreover, there is no room for how you would be judged for whatever you do. You have transcended all the barriers of the Body Mind. This is a world where the real you and the limitless world of the soul are at play to create your very own magic. While this magic will be manifested, witnessed, and put to use in the world of space, time, and limitations, it was crafted in a world of limitlessness.

This is the reality of great thinkers, researchers, and creators who do pathbreaking work to push the boundaries of what is already known to the world of the Body Mind. This explains the clarity and conviction behind the paths some chosen people pick early in their journeys, defying the rules, laws, or conditioning of the material instinct.

EMOTION MANAGEMENT: THE HUB AND SPOKE MODEL OF HUMAN EMOTIONS

In our human experience, we tide through various emotions—the good ones and the not-so-good ones. We may all desire a perfect and happy world where we are untouched by emotional discomfort, yet the truth is that life would be incredibly staid without the spice of emotions. Most of us take stock of life and the void we feel only when we experience a massive emotional upheaval. Emotions, thus, are vital for us to evolve in our spiritual journey.

However, where do these positive and negative emotions emanate from? We can find the answer in the most overwhelming feeling that forms the basis of our existence—love.

Love remains the predominant emotion in our early years until the influences start to work on the soul and corrupt it. Many of us find ourselves trapped in a state where extreme emotions start dancing in our heads and manage the way we feel. The love nucleus, in several instances, can be severely compromised to a point where it gets manhandled by negative emotions, taking over our captaincy. It is ironic that we are the actual gatekeepers of our purity, yet we allow these negative emotions to dominate us.

We need to be conscious of the potential onslaught of these negative waves and recognise how to deal with them. As mentioned earlier, we are humans and will experience a whole spectrum of emotions. Again, we need to discern between being subservient to emotional onslaughts or being a witness with the management capability to deal with these nasty currents.

Wherever you might be in your current capacity as an emotions manager, we will help you deconstruct this fascinating world of emotions and offer you some tactical power tools to deal with a potential onslaught of negative emotions caused by a stubborn stimulus.

We nudge you to use your 'Vitamin Love Index' score from Chapter 3 to understand your current love quotient. Your score in the assessment would have been closer to 50 for you to function from a fuller love hub. On the other hand, if your score is closer to 250, you are in the grip of a depleted love centre.

Your current score is the starting point for you to truly understand the reasons behind the intensity of the emotions you might experience. Once again, our conditioning during our formative years determines the 'Vitamin Love' score we operate from. This index is the invisible force behind all our outward emotional manifestations.

We will now delve deeper to understand the impact of the love index on how we treat ourselves emotionally. This can be explained by simply illustrating the hub and spoke model of emotions (*see illustration on next page*).

Love—being our soul nature—transcends all other feelings and emotions, sitting at the hub of our emotional balance. Imagine each spoke to be an emotion, coming together to form the wheel of emotions. These spokes of emotion stem from the love hub where an interesting dynamic is at play between the hub and the spokes. If the love hub is in a state of depletion, the individual would be naturally vulnerable to an onslaught of negative emotions. Any minor stimulus can have one spinning in an emotional turmoil, forget what happens if the stimulus is substantive. In this situation,

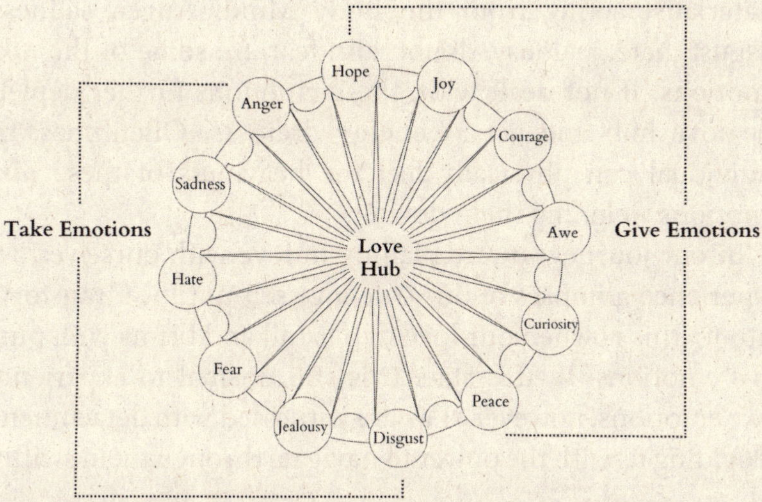

The Wheel of Emotions

even the positive emotions are stunted as they stem from a depleted heart. On the contrary, if we make efforts to keep our love hub full, we will experience long-lasting and full-hearted positive emotions. Our negative emotions would be swiftly dealt with, making them short-lived. In other words, the nature and intensity of our emotions are a direct function of the state of our love hub.

Give and Take Emotions

Positive emotions like joy, courage, hope, awe, curiosity, gratitude, and peace can also be called 'give emotions'. These are fuelled by love at the core and are carriers of the happy chemicals that blend with our blood to keep us feeling and performing well. The other basket of emotions is known as 'take emotions', which stem from our ego, attachment, and expectations. These are the typical traits of a mindless materialist acting from the Body Mind. Anger, sadness, disgust, hate, jealousy, doubt, and fear are some of the *take* emotions. If not dealt with, these emotions further deplete the love hub and act as energy drainers. Oftentimes, an individual can physically feel the heaviness of these *take* emotions weighing them down.

In our journey towards falling in love with ourselves, we experience glimpses of our true love self until we transform into it. This is when our love hub is full and brims with pure *give* emotions. In this state it is still normal to experience *take* emotions, however, they are witnessed with detachment, providing us with the power to navigate through them swiftly.

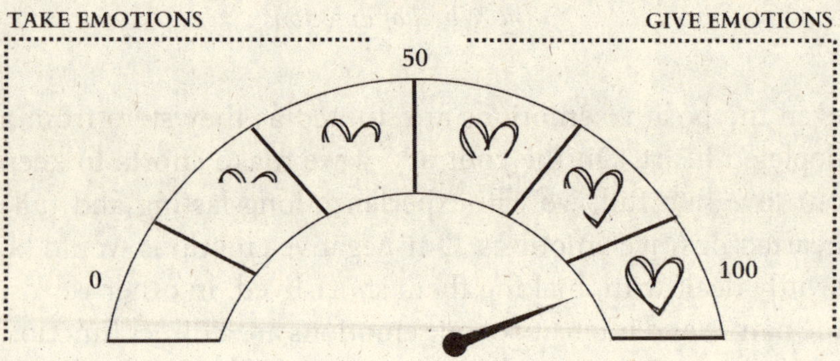

The Relationship between the Emotions and the Love Hub

Let us look at the dynamics of emotions using a simple mathematical model. Consider 100 as the index of our love hub, which means that, at the index of 100, we are in our natural state of being completely in love with ourselves. Here, we emanate the purest form of love in all our *give* emotions. These positive emotions, originating from a 100-index love hub, will have us overflowing with love. With every effort to fill our love hub or move closer to the 100 index, we increase our capacity to experience and share the *give* emotions in their purest form.

On the other side of the equation, assume we are currently sitting on an index of 30 on our love hub. At this level, we are in a naturally depleted state and will be drawn towards negativity and *take* emotions. It would require minimal introspection to come to terms with this reality.

In this case, the only option for us would be to either get sucked into the quicksand of the low index or to recognise the void and make a conscious effort to fill it with love.

Mentioned below is a tactical tool that will help you tide over tough emotional moments, releasing *take* emotions.

Drain Cleansing Programme for Take Emotions

To deepen our connection with the love centre, it is crucial to manage and release our draining *take* emotions. The drain cleansing programme takes us through the vital stages of knowing, accepting, decoding, and flushing the stimulus causing negative emotions. Here, we will only focus on dealing with the most overpowering *take* emotion experienced by everyone—fear.

For instance, when fear hits us because of a health scare, we begin treating the symptoms of unease with minuscule attention to the root cause of the fear. These symptoms and the diagnosis can stir a negative emotional turmoil in our mind and body. This state of panic leads us in the direction of medical treatment; however, the ongoing and never-ending emotional turmoil damages us.

The fundamental problem with this approach is that we forget to understand the real stimulus of this fear and focus on treating the superficial symptoms. Most importantly, nothing is done about dealing with the emotional onslaught. The problem with this approach is that we only use our conditioned Body Mind as the main strategic thinker. We are unaware of our access to the most loving and supremely intelligent doctor within us, our Soul Mind. We forget that the Soul Mind possesses the supreme power to heal our troubled Body Mind and the stimulus causing this havoc.

In our approach to dealing with the stimulus, we use the power and capability of the Body and Soul Mind, which can have miraculous results. If we revisit the example where we identified a case of intense fear caused by the onset of an illness, we will realise that it is wiser to confront both the trigger and the emotional and physical symptoms at the same time. Until we address this trigger, we will never be able to eliminate the symptoms. In most cases, if we adopt the right approach to deal with the stimulus, the need to treat the symptoms will gradually disappear.

The drain cleansing programme consists of four important steps, which we will apply to the *take* emotion of fear and understand how it can get us on the path to our natural state of balance and peace.

Step 1: Awareness of the Stimulus

When fear invades the mind, observe it and allow it to express itself. Try to understand the source of your fear that can, consciously or unconsciously, guide your patterns and behaviours. A powerful technique to help you get to grips with the source of fear is the 'peeling of layers' exercise. It is a self-discovery tool that can help you peel the layers to get to the root cause of the problem. Whenever you have an episode of fearfulness, take a deep breath and ask yourself, w*hy am I* *feeling fear in this situation?* With every response you receive, go deeper and get to the root of the problem with probing 'why' questions. Keep digging until you are convinced you have been able to isolate the culprit.

A large percentage of individuals struggle with the uncertainty surrounding the cause of their fear, and identifying the root cause is half the battle won. Below is a framework to assist you in peeling back the layers for yourself.

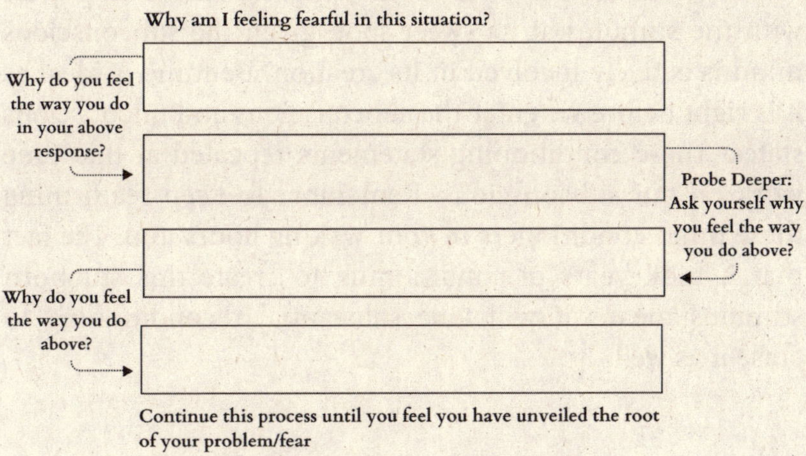

Exercise: Peeling the Layers

Step 2: Acceptance and Mind Conditioning

Accepting the presence of a fear-inducing stimulus is critical to healing. The more we deny the living truth of the triggers, the fiercer it becomes. Even though it seems momentarily convenient and easier to brush things under the carpet, it is wiser to bite the bullet and accept its presence.

Once accepted, it is time to condition our minds to deal with the stimulus. To do so, the mind needs to be prepared. This preparation can begin with the repetitive use of simple mind conditioners. Genuinely feel and believe these mind conditioners to overcome the barriers depleting your love hub. Don't say what you want to believe; believe what you want to say.

Think of these as positive currents we send to our mind to prepare for a phase of fundamental correction at the source. In effect, these conditioning statements are designed to help repair our damaged love hub. The best time to internalise these mind conditioners is when we hit the sack. This timing deals with the stimulus at its sweet spot, given the subconscious mind is actively involved in its creation. Bedtime is ideal as it is right before we enter the subconscious and unconscious states. These conditioning statements repeated at this time work on our subconscious. Remember to keep reaffirming these mind conditioners in your waking hours, too. The fact that it took years of conditioning to create this stubborn stimulus means it will take substantial reconditioning to erase it as well.

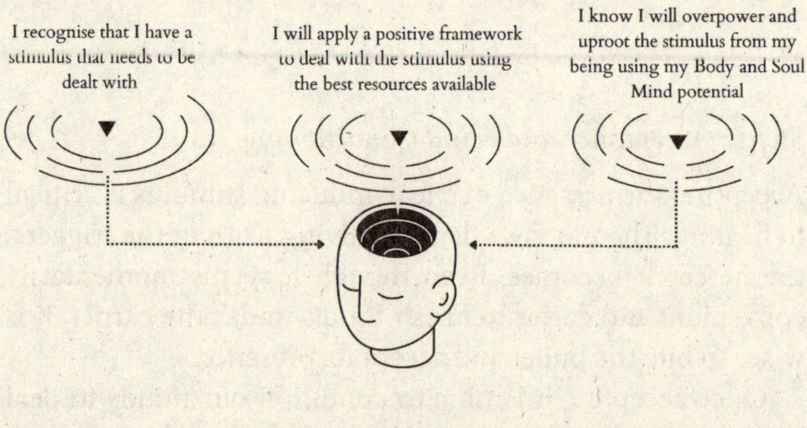

Mind Conditioners

Step 3: The Practical Approach

When we are conditioned with positivity, it is time to deal with the issue using our practical mind. This step must be invoked if the intensity of the situation and damage caused by the stimulus require professional and medical expertise. Head in the direction of doctors, ayurveda specialists, naturopaths, mental health professionals, and anyone else you might think of as domain experts who can guide you in planning your fight against the problem.

Based on the advice you receive and want to follow, narrow down the imperatives and act on them swiftly.

Step 4: Draining the Stimulus—The Flush Approach

Once the symptoms have been addressed, initiate a parallel process to flush out the thought of the stimulus and the emotional turmoil that accompanies it. This is where the Soul Mind comes in, acting as a natural counsellor to maintain our body's well-being. We condition the mind to flush the existence of the stimulus from our system, using the Soul Mind to witness the emotional turmoil from a distance and bring our Body Mind closer to its natural state of peace.

Along the way, we must apply principles of mind control to use positive emotions to help eliminate the stimulus and the consequent emotional upheaval. By training our mind to untie the knot causing the fear, we create an environment that can potentially dissolve the stimulus at its source, as if it never existed.

The flush approach is a mind-resetting technique designed to extinguish the fear-inducing stimulus within. We condition our mind both during meditation and in other waking moments to imagine the stimulus as non-existent.

Achieving a state where we believe in the non-existence of the stimulus will naturally extinguish the emotional turmoil and rebuild positive emotional currents to heal the body and mind.

In other words, this approach trains our mind to view the triggers from the perspective of the Soul Mind, where at the level of the soul nothing can affect us.

Let us apply this process to an illness diagnosis. After addressing the diagnosis with appropriate medical advice, avoid worrying about it, as it will only fuel the fire. Use the flush approach, with your Soul Mind, to believe in the non-existence of the illness. This will help create positive healing energy in your body and mind. From a Soul Mind perspective, we are body-free and hence disease-free.

MIND MATTERS IN RELATIONSHIPS

By now we have a clearer understanding of how our emotions affect us and our relationships. In fact, our emotional health can have a direct impact on the quality of our relationships. *Take* emotions deplete and strain our relationships while *give* emotions naturally nourish our relationships.

As we get caught up in the chase, it is almost impossible to not get victimised by *take* emotions. Ego, insecurity, selfishness, or jealousy weaken the foundation of our relationships. As we embrace the true spirit of being love, we free ourselves from the toxins of expectations, overdependence, overattachment, and neediness, resulting in unhealthy relationships. In this state, we build on relationships powered by love, ensuring they are mutually enriching.

As we ascend from material to freedom, from Body Mind to Soul Mind, we witness an evolution in our relationships as well. We have laid down the ladder of evolution in relationships as we uncover and embrace our true loving selves.

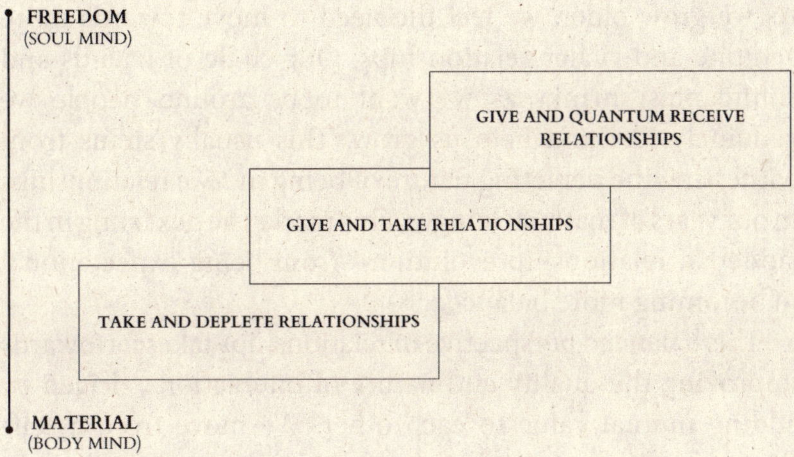

Evolution in Relationships

Take and Deplete Relationships

At the bottom rung, we have relationships built on an overtly expectational instinct, where we take without feeling the need to give back. Most people in the material plane operating from a Body Mind state thrive in this *take* ecosystem. Somewhere, the material benefit we can derive from our relationships fuels our investment in them and creates an invisible trap. Even in our most intimate bonds with our parents, siblings, or partners, the *take* mindset creeps in, depleting the quality of our interactions and causing disharmony that can lead to a potential fallout. We are so dependent on this breed of bonds that every response that does not conform to the expectation causes stress. This is a trap where we unconsciously give the key to our happiness to others and look at the naivety of it all.

Give and Take Relationships

As we grow older, we feel the need to move towards more genuine and richer relationships. Our circle of friends and confidantes shrinks as we want to be around people we genuinely like and help us grow. This usually stems from witnessing the depleting nature of being in *take* relationships in our years of material hunger. This marks the next rung in the ladder of relationship evolution—from being expectational to becoming more balanced.

This balanced perspective in relationships takes us towards improving the quality and nature of interactions, driven by adding mutual value to each other. We move from a self-focus to a more practical give-and-take approach. What's in it for 'me' transforms into how we can help each other. In this state, there is a lot more compassion towards nurturing relationships. The degree of love in our relationships increases, leading to a karmic reciprocation.

We are not completely devoid of having expectations in this rung of the ladder. At this stage, even after building a strong connection, we can feel a sense of disappointment when we don't receive what we expected. This loss can push us towards the lowest rung of the ladder. The key here is to build a more forgiving mindset towards a loss in expectations. While we may not see the effect of this mindset immediately, we will see it in time. We can build a more forgiving mindset by activating our Soul Mind thinking to forgive and release emotions and draining experiences.

Here begins our journey to evolving into better beings who are more in love with ourselves and others. Once we see the beauty of a richer relationship principle evolve, we have an inner unconscious yearning to keep attracting a higher quality of meaningful and mentally enriching relationships. The love factor starts to spread its magic. We tend to fall in love with this new need to love more.

Give and Quantum-Receive Relationships

The ultimate experience of freedom in relationships arises when we are in a Soul Mind state and have completely shed our expectations from others. There are no selfish pursuits, only purity in giving and serving with unconditional love and joy. The fulfilment experienced in contributing to another's happiness is at the heart of this highest rung of the relationship ladder.

In this phase, we also become more understanding of the reasons behind others' behaviour. This understanding makes us respond differently, lovingly, and positively to any situation and help others transcend their challenges.

Such individuals are self-aware, self-content, and brimming with self-love. Once we reach this stage, we stop assigning badges to people as a filter to decide how to treat them. Humans, animals, and the environment are seen as beautiful forms of nature meant to be loved. This is a world of abundant love, the kind we crave but eludes us in the take phase of our evolution.

We must be mindful that, at this stage, love might warrant tough responses, especially when we are up against a situation or an individual that requires a forceful response. All actions inspired by love need not be loving on the surface. In this highest state of giving, our intention behind the action is always for the ultimate good of the individual or the situation involved. For the right reasons, silence, controlled firmness, confrontation, withdrawal, or even indifference can be expressions of our love. For instance, a mother could use controlled firmness to make a disrespecting child understand the virtue of kindness.

The phenomenon of giving selflessly involves an interesting karmic dimension—we effortlessly receive abundance at a quantum scale. This is an invisible equation at play that eludes most people who think logically. However, this phenomenon must be experienced to be believed. The nonattachment to results gives way to the vault of absolute abundance. The beauty of this approach is that we no longer chase after things or people. Instead, by focusing on our path, we naturally attract what we desire, and others begin to seek us out.

6.3
Spiritual Body: Raising Consciousness

'We are not human beings having a spiritual experience; we are spiritual beings having a human experience.'
—Pierre Teilhard de Chardin

Various religions over the centuries have spoken about our soul state being immortal. Some religions talk further about reincarnation as a part of the never-ending journey of the soul until it reaches a stage of Nirvana. Independently, over the centuries, some evolved yogis spent much of their lives in meditation trying to uncover the secrets of the inner world. Their claims were not based on the esoteric beliefs of a select few heads of religious sects but rather on the inner science they experienced through deep meditation. Their only purpose was to transcend consciousness to higher levels, which they achieved. The most evolved and spiritually fired knowledge that exists on the subject today comes from the teachings of the yogis.

Over the centuries, material science has had a sceptic view of the claims of the spiritualists. All they believed in was everything that existed in the form of matter and relatability.

In this debate between the believers and the non-believers, progressive science got intrigued by the claims of the spiritualists. We believe that many of the astute research academicians have a robust human side to them. As they progress in their path-breaking research, the throbbing humanity-inspired questions get intertwined in the equation, leading them to go deeper into the spiritual realms.

Some of the main reasons for this shift in the scientific community include documented experiences of people, especially children, remembering past lives—independently authenticated by the authorities—as well as recorded near-death experiences and past-life regression revelations under the supervision of trained therapists.

The science of quantum physics is based on newer discoveries of everything being a form of energy, fundamentally non-local and uncontainable in physical form. This new science has opened a whole new and fascinating field of research and discoveries that are progressively unearthing the claims of spiritualists. The good news is that in most instances, the spiritualists were right.

We will now venture into the invisible world full of abstractness where we delve deep into searching for our truth. This real yet often forgotten world is lost to us during our formative years, giving way to artificiality. This part of the toolkit requires faith. Approach it with an open mind as we try to connect this abstract world with logic.

UNDERSTANDING YOUR NATURE

Our nature has a straightforward definition—it is a state of being where we live and engage selflessly from our heart, with a clear understanding of our purpose and free of any conditioning.

All actions emanating from our true nature have clarity, pure intent, simplicity, and love at the source. In our true essence, we are full of joy, selflessness, love, kindness, compassion, and equanimity for ourselves and everything around us. This is a mind space where we realise we are nature ourselves, deeply interconnected with the nature around us.

How many of us can honestly say that we understand our nature and are being true to it?

We are all unique human beings gifted by nature to do exceptional things. However, the hyper-organisation of the modern world pressurises us, making us believe in the glitter of set patterns and herd thinking. This may be the reason for the minuscule number of people who choose their passion as a profession compared to going after conventional career options that guarantee financial and ego security.

We are programmed to believe that financial security and prosperity must be the goal of our lives and source of happiness. In this illusion, we move away from creating our purpose, losing sight of our real selves in this mad chase of a man-made truth.

Power Tool: Imagination

Imagine a world thousands of years ago where people were surrounded by nature. There were no educational institutions, organisations, countries, marriages, or rules and regulations to contextualise our existence. In this world, people only had to live in nature, with their nature. In that world, individuals chose to do what came to them intuitively, and relationships were not categorised methodically. The world at that point included looking for food from the natural surroundings and the occupations included creatively harnessing nature using resources like mud or wood to name a few. That must have been a world with much love and contentment and the least animosity and greed.

Returning to our source requires us to imagine ourselves in this prehistoric world. The nature-to-nature connection needs to be imagined in its pure and undiluted setting. Ask yourself: What activities am I naturally drawn towards in this prehistoric setting? This may throw light on leanings like a quest to grow food in a more organised manner or harness wood to make spears to hunt or create works of art using resources like mud.

Once you identify the source of your natural yearning, shift your consciousness from prehistoric times to the current times. Imagine how your inclination would play out in today's context, given the technology-driven world we live in. This is a simple yet effective exercise that will help you find your archetype. Some examples of these archetypes are abundance, which in today's context could mean running a commercial business; love—doing work for the love of people; power—running communities of people as a leader; or healing—being a doctor or alternate healer in today's context.

This introspection will guide you through profound soul-searching and provide some clarity on how far you have strayed from your true nature. In short, it may help you reconnect with your innate direction, filled with creativity and love.

UNDERSTANDING CONSCIOUSNESS

In our human experience, the most important school that we go to is the school of life. This is no formal school like we understand in conventional terms. This is the school we create in our minds, pushing us to learn and grow in our understanding of this miracle called life. This intrigue of understanding these deep secrets kicks in for different people at distinct times. These moments of inquiry are induced either by natural curiosity or an incident that pushes us to think harder.

Once the quest to unravel the truth takes hold of us, it begins to grow. With its growth comes a new understanding and perspective of our real story, extending into the world of consciousness. This quest involves understanding and becoming aware of the different levels of consciousness, starting with the ones we experience daily, and progressing up the ladder into transcendental states. For most of us, the intrigue around our experiential states of consciousness, which are the subconscious and unconscious, is a part of the open eye world of relatability. These two states are experienced daily with little or no attention to what is happening and as a function of them being a part of our everyday reality.

Seeking our deeper states of being serves as a gateway to opening pathways for the higher transcendental states of consciousness. These transcendental states have been the crux of meditation by yogis in tough living conditions over centuries. This lot of inner technologists who research these deeper realms have just one purpose in life—to keep going deeper within and without.

In the 1960s, a curious academician from Harvard University conducted experiments to understand these transcendental states. His focus was to study the higher states of consciousness experienced using lifestyle drugs like LSD. He was aware that our minds can experience heightened states of consciousness. However, the route to the experiment was a convenient shortcut to deep meditation. This clarifies the real reason for the large numbers of people addicted to substance abuse as a shortcut to the experience-heightened states of awareness. The leader of this experiment eventually embraced the path of yoga and became an accomplished sanyaasi, popularly known as Baba Ram Dass.

These higher states of transcendence have been a subject of research for several faculties in academics over the years. Cutting-edge research in quantum physics, pure mathematics, and medical sciences have all been working on exploring this deep predicament that could open our minds to unthinkable new frontiers. This research has, like Dr Richard Alpert (alias Baba Ram Dass), led to research academicians following the path of spirituality to make the connection.

The scientific community continues to investigate the yogis' claims about the immortality of the soul and the truth of soul consciousness. Meanwhile, spiritualists delve deeper into the subject, enriching their lives with experiential wisdom and miraculous experiences.

For those on the path of inner awakening, the scientific method to experience this evolution of consciousness is through the constant practice of meditation under the guidance of evolved spiritual masters.

Decoding the States of Consciousness

The waking awareness that we experience with all our senses from moment to moment is what we call our world of existence. Under the illusion of what we absorb, with our senses, we create our life stories. This state sits at the gross level in the spacetime world of consciousness. This is the truth of our lives in our limited comprehension.

The other two states of consciousness we witness are the subconscious and the unconscious. We experience these states daily with no real attention to them. As we experience these states with full attention, we start our journey into the deeper recesses of understanding the subtler levels of consciousness.

Our quest eventually leads us to unravel the invisible deeper truths of the soul consciousness. This search for our soul state of mind takes us on a journey beyond the physical and mental confines of our human form. This is our true eternal state beyond space or time.

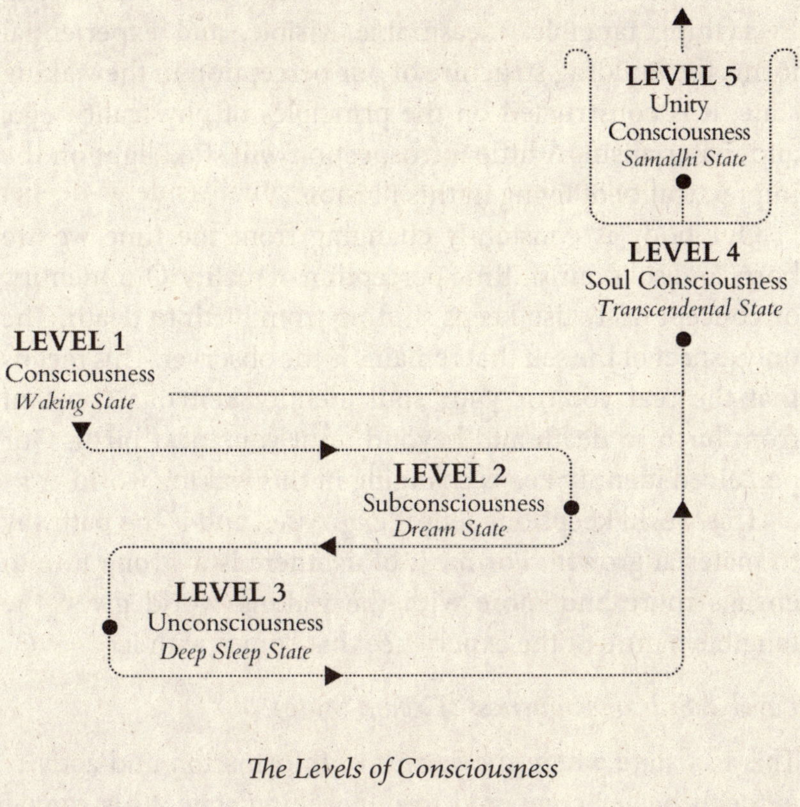

The Levels of Consciousness

Let us explore these states in more detail.

Level 1: Consciousness (Waking State)

At the most apparent level, we are all aware of and experience consciousness. This phenomenon of what we experience as the present-moment awareness is what we relate to as consciousness. We soak in our knowledge of the now through all our senses. In other words, from the moment we awaken to the moment we sleep, we are in a waking state of consciousness.

We become so involved in the waking state and everything material that accompanies it, we call this our world. Everything tangible, measurable, visible, and experiential forms the building structure of our perception in the waking state. It is constructed on the principles of physicality, ego, and materialism. A little introspection will shed light on the impracticality of living in this illusion.

Our body is constantly changing from the time we are born, and so is our shifting perception of reality. Our identity, or concept of 'I', also keeps shifting from birth to death. The only aspect of the self that remains is the observer. This means that the real you, or your soul identity, remains constant from birth to death and beyond until your next birth. Our perceived identity keeps changing in this waking world.

This world keeps our senses engrossed and is the pathway to material growth. For most of us, there is a strong lure to engage more and more with the waking world given the tangible nature of the experience that comes with it.

Level 2: Subconsciousness (Dream State)

This is a state where the canvas of information and activity is much bigger compared to our waking state. This canvas not only stores all our conditioning or programming from the early years but is also the hotbed of limitless creativity, information, and knowledge.

The programming stored in our subconscious makes us operate in conditioned ways in our waking time. This is also the state we slip into when we go to sleep until we reach deep sleep. This is our state of the dreaming mind.

We often dream about relatable people and issues or completely fantasy-driven themes. This is a world of unbounded imagination, often inspired by the experiences of the waking world. Threads from our conscious and subconscious reality seep into the tapestry of our dreams. If we are going through a negative phase in life, it tends to influence our dreams and vice versa. Unresolved trauma or suppressed emotions also express themselves in our dreams. There could be great learnings or cues waiting to be discovered in these dreams. All we need is to be mindful.

The subconscious state, in effect, is a treasure trove that we often ignore as we go about our lives. The moment we wake up to the vastness and nature of this great mind bank, we awaken to the reality of how vital a role it can play in our journey of self-correction.

Level 3: Unconsciousness (Deep Sleep State)

This is a state where we draw an absolute blank—a state of total nothingness with no noise from the waking or the dream state. We experience unconsciousness every day in the form of deep sleep. The only other time we go through it is when we become unconscious due to a medical issue. This is a state of bliss where we have no memory, yet we crave it daily in the form of deep sleep.

This experience of unconsciousness is the closest to how we feel in heightened states of meditation that lead to Samadhi. This is our real eternal home—our soul state of mind.

Imagine if we could live the waking state as if it felt like deep sleep—a state of mind that is calm and has zero thought in the waking world.

Level 4: Soul Consciousness (Transcendental State)

While we are accustomed to interacting with the outer world, we often forget that there is an inner world within us—our real self or our true nature, which is pure love, free from external influences. This state of consciousness is experienced at the level of the soul, where we exist beyond physicality, space, or time.

In this state, we traverse an abstract and non-scientific reality, experiencing the knowledge that we are not limited by the body and mind. We feel a detachment between the true self and our physical form. This detachment allows us to experience freedom, flow, and the potential for miraculous possibilities, without fear.

Understanding the concept of soul consciousness, which is not confined to the body, opens up infinite possibilities. The soul can achieve the impossible and create miracles. Our physical world transforms into a limitless realm full of wonder and newness, where nothing is impossible, and dreams do come true. This state is known as *Turiya* in yogic terminology, the transcendental fourth stage of consciousness.

Through meditation, we grow in our understanding and experience of transitioning from consciousness to soul consciousness. This requires significant practice and a genuine desire to achieve it. Initially, we experience soul consciousness in brief glimpses, witnessing our awareness.

As we witness the unimaginable power and peace of this state, we naturally yearn for longer periods of this mind state. As we grow in our meditation practice towards this fourth state, we become witnesses of our conscious, subconscious, and unconscious phases.

A practical tool to move closer to Soul Mind consciousness in everyday situations involves training our minds to think and process information from a Soul Mind perspective. By filtering our thoughts through the lens of the soul—centred in love, immortality, and invulnerability—we become invincible. In any situation, we can step back, be a witness, and consider how our Soul Mind would process an experience. When the Body Mind receives answers from the Soul Mind, it can rationalise the benefits of using the Soul Mind filter, allowing us to align with the Soul Mind rather than being trapped in the ego-driven Body Mind.

To help you on your journey to awaken your Soul Mind, we will introduce the 'going back to source' framework, which uses contemplative meditation techniques. This powerful tool called the Soul Mind kriya will help you access your true soul self. While we share this technique to help you on your path, it is important to note that achieving a permanent soul state requires the guidance of evolved yogis or spiritual masters.

Internalising the concept of soul consciousness requires true surrender to the idea of a soul home and the existence of a soul. Faith is a precursor to experiencing this existence. Through this journey of working on your physical, mental, and spiritual bodies, you will gain clarity about your *Prakriti* and eventually your purpose in life. A soul-conscious person is naturally enveloped in love, attracting people and elements of nature. You will emanate love through your intentions and actions, experiencing spiritual magnetism that should be used responsibly to give back wholeheartedly.

Level 5: Unity Consciousness (Samadhi State)

Highly evolved yogis or spiritual masters who commit lifetimes in deep meditation, evolving in their understanding of the ultimate truth, move from being soul-conscious to a part of unity consciousness. This is a state of Samadhi or enlightenment, the ultimate state for any human being to achieve and the goal of their spiritual journeys.

In this state, we are fully aware of the presence of a world filled with other souls. This parallel universe exists based on the principles of soul consciousness, where we witness a soul in everything and everybody. We can look at a flower at the physical level while also communicating with the flower at the soul level. We become aware of our past lives and ancestors in this beautiful world that thrives on love.

The evolved souls can communicate with the soul of whoever or whatever they want, making the impossible happen. This is popularly known as the s*iddhi*, *the* power of the yogis where they can make miracles happen. However, these miracles are a matter of science to the yogis.

This is the living reality of the revered and truly enlightened spiritual masters. The transcendental journey of moving from consciousness to soul consciousness and beyond needs to be undertaken with the guidance of such learnt masters. The moment we develop an inner yearning to evolve in our levels of consciousness, we naturally feel the need to be guided on this path. This is where our search for a guru begins.

Some people have left high-paying corporate jobs to pursue their spiritual paths. There are also stories of individuals embarking on a journey to find spiritual guidance, meeting various spiritual leaders before choosing one to follow. Remember this: On this journey, your intuition will guide you towards the right master. This is also dependent on which master wants you to come under their tutelage. Under the guidance of an evolved spiritual master, your journey in the spirit world could lead you to witness new worlds.

This fascinating field of understanding the subtler states of consciousness is also an area of deep study in the field of quantum sciences. They are trying to catch up with the spiritual mysteries of the East to uncover the truth of soul and unity consciousness.

The discoveries in quantum sciences are beginning to uncover the energy facet of everything and everyone. This means an invisible energy aspect exists in all things, and energies interact in a non-local context. In simpler terms, the theory of space-time and the necessity of a physical signal for communication between entities are being challenged.

This exciting field of research has opened a new realm where interactions occur beyond the physical world. It is a realm of possibilities driven by the discovery of signal-less energy interaction outside the space-time continuum, where there is no space, no time, only pure potentiality.

This is the world of unity consciousness, where everything and everyone is connected at the level of energy or soul. In this world, any pure thought energy emitted by an individual can attract relevant energies through quantum entanglement. The interconnectedness extends to the energy from the Sun, oxygen from the trees, food from the crops, and the people we interact with, all seen as interconnected at the energy level.

As science increasingly aligns with ancient wisdom, people worldwide are becoming intrigued and drawn to unravel their true soul stories.

THE SOUL MIND KRIYA

We have devoted a significant part this book to uncovering the power of self-love in guiding us back to our true nature. This involves working comprehensively on our physical, mental, and spiritual bodies. We have provided effective tools for your Body Mind to start searching for your Soul Mind. The tools and techniques shared thus far allow us to experience Soul Mind in glimpses. Now, we will share a structured 'going back to source' framework that can be personalised to help you get closer to your Soul Mind more frequently.

The Soul Mind kriya is a unique meditation technique that helps you transcend into thinking like a sanyaasi. It will guide you from wherever you are on the Vitamin Love Index to a fuller love hub and will use contemplative meditation techniques to clean the dust off the sheath of your pure self. Transcending your consciousness from the level of your body to your Soul is the fundamental quest of your journey to freedom. What differentiates the Soul Mind kriya from other meditation techniques is its foundation in relatability and inner contemplation of your personal experiences. This involves being led by your intuition, giving you the power to peel back the layers and find your true self.

This life-altering phenomenon of achieving a state of Soul Mind thinking is based in the abstract sphere. The idea is to make it relatable so people can make sense of it. This kriya provides an easy, methodical, and logical breakdown of the process.

There is enough scientific evidence to support how meditation can alter the creation of brain waves, changing the levels of activity in the brain. When one understands the journey of the brain waves from prebirth to the later years, one can logically relate to the Soul Mind kriya.

This technique helps individuals understand the evolution of their brain from the point of energy or wave creation and the invisible effect of their unconscious programming on the nature and frequency of these waves. Using this understanding, we will guide you through a process that will help you move from a cluttered or thought-heavy mind full of programming to a state of zeroness, as in prebirth.

This process starts by unravelling the subconscious mind by pushing aside our analytical mind, which operates in the waking world. We need to access and witness the canvas of our subconscious, which is much larger than our waking world. Using a combination of images, emotions, and perceptions of our earlier memories, the Soul Mind kriya will help you unearth your invisible programming. In other words, consistent contemplation in meditation will allow us to reflect minutely on all the distinct phases of our lives that were instrumental in the code creation that was cemented into our subconscious. Once the subconscious programming becomes clear, we use our time in meditation and other waking moments to heal the defining circumstances that led to the code creation. This will essentially require reinforcing love, unshakeable and eternity-inspired thoughts from a distilled Soul Mind perspective as a healing balm over the trigger.

This practice may bring moments of doubt and disbelief, but the key is to stay focused. This process involves recognising the effect of materialism on our lives and how we were programmed to respond from this inner software. As we see the code at play, we can get to the root of our issues. Just as the inner software took years to cement in our subconscious, the erasing will also take time.

We need to address all important aspects of our lives that have been corroded by the material world. Once aware of this compromised inner coding, we need to make a conscious effort to erase it by creating energy inspired by love, not materialism. This code must be readdressed in phases, identifying clear slivers of importance called the components of the code and must be dealt with one at a time. For instance, if you had to take a closer look at the component of professional choice, you could undo the conditioning that led you to become an engineer and instead listen to your inner nature to pursue what you love, which could be farming.

As we progress in our kriya practice, we will notice why we did what we did at various stages that took us away from our real selves. Awakening to this awareness will begin the process of erasing the code. Using thought reinforcement inspired by love to erase and replace the code is potent enough to help us cope with disease using the power of our minds.

As we erase our subconscious programming, we will begin to see our inner self in glimpses. This is the ultimate step in this kriya, where we push our programmed subconscious mind aside to make room for our true selves.

The real you is like a ball of light, brightest in early years. Those nurtured to stay in their true form retain their natural luminosity and grow up to script great stories. Others, conditioned by the material world, live fundamentally stunted stories. This conditioning sits like a sheath of dust on your light, diminishing its luminosity and preventing the source light from powering your inner light. As you erase the code in your subconscious, you make way for the source light to seep in. This happens in phases, and you witness more source light with each erasure. When you completely erase the muddy sheath, you become one with the source, and your Soul Mind becomes part of the universal or supreme consciousness.

This kriya will take you on a journey of reverse engineering your minds to return to the source. To understand this reverse journey, it is important to unearth the framework of wave creation and programming at the various stages of our lives.

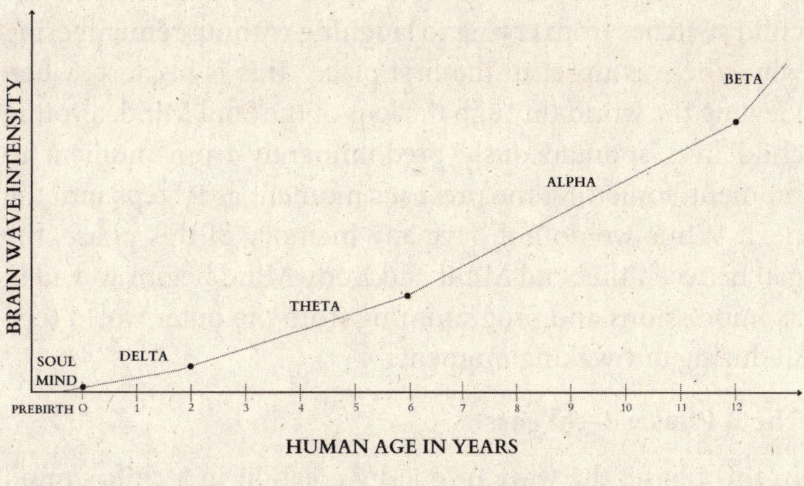

The Framework of Wave Creation over Time

Prebirth: Pure Soul Mind Consciousness

During the nine-month phase of pregnancy, the soul enters the foetus's body. A baby in the womb rests in a mind space of nothingness and pure love which is the nature of our soul. Our Soul Mind in this new body is on the cusp of starting a new life of impressions, with zero conscious memory of the lives gone by. The foetus has near zero brain wave activity. This is our natural functioning state from the Soul Mind. In this phase, our Body Mind is still in the process of being manufactured. Another way to look at our mind state during this phase is that the Soul Mind is essentially at the seat of the Body Mind.

Delta Phase: 0–2 Years

In the first two years of our lives, our mind operates at its slowest pace in terms of wave creation. During this phase, the mind of the soul dominates the perception of reality. A child switches from crying to laughing without remembering why s/he was upset in the first place. This is because, when viewing the world through the lens of the Soul Mind, a young child lives spontaneously predominantly from moment to moment, forgetting the previous moment as it steps into the next. While we do not have any memory of this phase, the gap between the Soul Mind and Body Mind begins to widen as impressions and programming from the outer world seep in during our waking moments.

Theta Phase: 2–6 Years

In this phase, the wave or energy creation in a child's mind surges, making it the years of fantasy. Most of the time spent during these years is driven by curiosity and imagination, creating an atmosphere akin to a fantasy story. These are also the years where we experience a great deal of subconscious preconditioning, where future reference programming is being unconsciously written.

Thus, we refer to this phase as impressionable years. The preconditioning involves picking up signals of whom to love and whom not to, what to eat and what not to, whom to make friends with and whom not with, what to play and what to avoid, what to chase and what not to, and what to fear and what not to. However, these are only a few components of the code. This code will unknowingly become the ultimate guidebook we will use to respond to any stimulus later in life.

Conscious parents will be mindful of keeping their child as close to their love source as possible. This form of parenting encourages a child to explore and express their true nature. The truth, however, is that most of us download our conditioned world views onto our children, robbing them of their true selves.

This highlights the critical importance of parental care during formative years as a significant determinant of future outcomes. Therefore, all parents at this stage of their journey are gently encouraged to prioritise sowing the seeds of love as the foundation of all teachings and behaviours.

Alpha Phase: 6–12 Years

This is a phase where fantasy makes room for reality. We participate in the real world and are fairly set in our subconscious software. At this stage, we are managed by this software without being aware of it.

These are the years of our early schooling where we interact with larger social groups. Here, multiple software programmes are at play based on the unique conditioning of each child, challenging some of our earlier programmes. This combination of learning cements our response mechanism to varied situations.

Here, the creation of brain waves is in surge mode, keeping us over-occupied. In this phase, the Body Mind takes the primary seat in managing our lives.

Beta Phase: 12+ Years

This is our world of absolute and practical reality. Our sense of logic and reasoning, and, most importantly, decision-making stems from the software now acting as our operating system. All our earlier conditioning has now created deep-rooted programmes that compel us to live a material life. Here, we unknowingly and repeatedly fall into the trap of desire where, despite its fulfilment, we find ourselves in a never-ending loop of chasing one yearning after the next.

Given the constant influx of tasks and goals, we hardly have a moment to pause. Our brains are working at full capacity, and there's never a dull moment in our conscious awareness.

The Moment of Reckoning: This phase consists of the ultimate excitement where we realise our dreams and see material results flowing in. The drug of material excitement is so potent that we want more of it at any cost. At some point, this mad chase forces us to rethink our programming. We search for methodologies to help us find our centre, heading in all directions from fitness to yoga to nutrition to ayurveda and meditation. While all the entry points place us on the path to finding our real selves, the pace and comprehensiveness of reaching the destination differ.

This point of reckoning is either motivated by a vacuum or incident or, for the wiser lot, can be a conscious move towards a truer life. This is where the Soul Mind kriya acts as a comprehensive power tool to begin your soul search.

This technique involves transitions from the Beta state of our mind, when we begin our meditation practice, to reach the Delta state. The ultimate quest is to reach the prebirth state of consciousness. The process starts by clearing the clutter associated with the Beta state and then consciously working on erasing the mental 'software programmes' that have been ingrained in our brains. This gradual journey progresses through the Alpha and Theta states, ultimately reaching Delta.

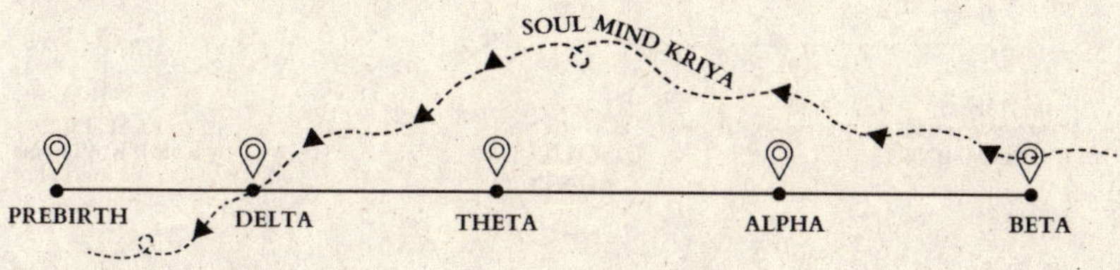

Reverse Engineering

This transition from Theta to Delta takes place in the more advanced stages of our meditative practice. We need to approach meditation with the view to achieve the mind state of a 0–2-year-old child. This seems relatable and doable, as we have experienced this state in our body form and can relate to getting there even though we have no memory of that phase.

This stage must be the ultimate quest of our meditative practice. In this headspace, we experience absolute stillness and awareness, well beyond our comprehension.

Design Your Soul-Search Master Plan

The process of going inwards involves understanding the two layers that surround us and keep us from being one with our source light. The outermost layer is our source energy, where we all exist as possibilities at the level of unity consciousness. The innermost layer is our Soul Mind, covered with the dust of subconscious programming and its ramifications. These ramifications of our subconscious code keep us excessively engaged in the waking world. We aim to erase this sheath of dust created by these two layers for the Soul Mind to merge with the light of the source.

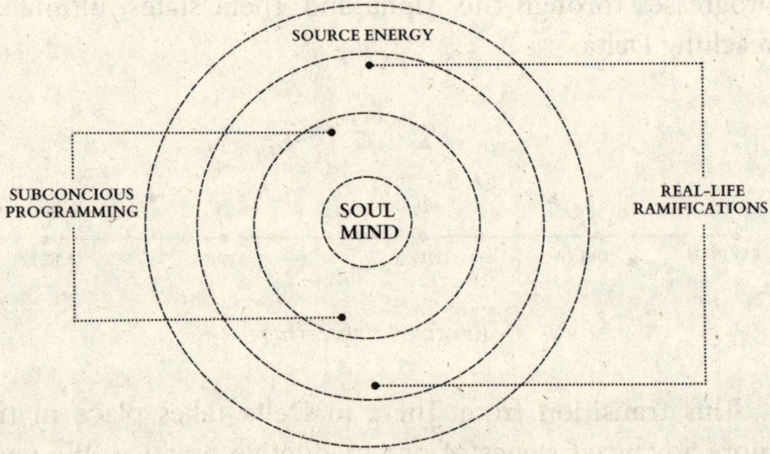

The Soul-Search Master Plan

Step 1: Identify the Vital Code Components or Genres of Your Life

Our soul search begins with working on the second layer of identifying the subconscious code components or genres that form the cornerstones of our journey. These vital genres of life can be emotions like love, fear, happiness, ego, and anger, or facets of life like education, profession, complexes, relationships, failure, sex, loss, nutrition, disease, and spirituality. These are the important genres for which we have pre-defined responses in our code.

Step 2: List Down the Real-World Ramifications of a Given Code Component

The next step is to unearth the real-life manifestations related to the concerned genre. This means that every identified component will have a few frequently occurring incidents to which we have fixed or conditioned responses. There is no creativity in responding to the stimulus, just programmed answers to these situations. For instance, our conditioned response to aggression may be to become even more aggressive. This templated response stems from our programming, providing no new input in our behaviour.

These manifestations can swing towards both sides of the spectrum, positive or negative. If the manifestations are negative, they clearly need work at the source to correct the wiring. Positive manifestations can also be graded, ranging from being completely inspired by love to all possibilities leading up to a fully love-inspired manifestation. Our real goal is to change the code in question for all manifestations that are not entirely inspired by love.

Take one code at a time and consider how that component has manifested in events that have evoked a templated reaction in your life. If we take one of the most important facets of our life—relationships—as an example, the negative manifestations could include dependency on others, control and manipulation, extreme jealousy or possessiveness, emotional manipulation, unrealistic expectations, inability to love wholeheartedly, or insecurity.

Alternatively, if you reflect on how the emotion of anger is creating an imbalance in your life, you might find yourself relating to one or more of the following manifestations. You may be prone to verbal or physical aggression, sarcasm, chronic irritability, constantly blaming others, having a victim mentality, or indulging in self-destructive behaviour.

In the exercise above, we first identified the genres and then listed the ramifications. However, there is an alternative method to approach this process. You can also perform the exercise in reverse, moving from real-life manifestations to code components. Once you have laid down all the material manifestations, you can group related issues into clusters that you feel originate from the same subconscious code component or genre. For instance, if you find yourself unapologetic in relationships, critical of others, and valuing others based on their professional or educational markers, deep contemplation will help you unearth the code, which, in this case, stems from the ego component.

Step 3: Repeat Step 2 for All Code Components to Create Your Soul Search Matrix

This list of manifestations needs to be drawn up for the entire group of code components. You will be surprised at the number of templated responses stored in your subconscious world. We will soon reach a point where we can articulate most of what is important to us in writing. You will be able to see the entire software programme as an observer. With the completion of this step, you will have managed to pen down the Body Mind perspective of your life thus far.

Find below a representative breakdown of the potential negative manifestations emanating from a vital code component. Please note that the same logic needs to be applied to all the other code components—that might not be listed below—which you deem important in shaping your journey so far.

Code Component	Real World Manifestations (Negative)
Ego	• Attaching self-worth to wealth, fame, good looks, or achievements • Being critical of others • Lack of humility • Need for control • Arrogance and overconfidence • Undue defensiveness • Need for validation • Lack of empathy; self centredness • Difficulties in relationships • Rigidity and inflexibility • Unrealistic expectations • Competitiveness and envy • Jealousy • Insecurity
Fears	• Procrastination • Constant worrying • Anxiety issues • Catastrophising • Social withdrawal • Difficulty in communication • Micromanagement • Overcautiousness • Avoidance of risk • Neglecting self-care

Code Component	Real World Manifestations (Negative)
Relationships	• Dependency on others • Control and manipulation • Extreme jealousy or possessiveness • Emotional manipulation • Unrealistic expectations • Inavility to love wholeheartedly • Inavility to express love • Insecurity • Propensity to escalate conflicts • Resentment; built-up baggage • Disregarding boundaries • Narcissism • Selfishness • Transactional mindset • Poor communication • Avidance • Chronic disrespect • Constant criticism • Physical abuve • Mistrust
Happiness	• External achievements: money, position, power, validation • Perfectionism • Loving others over ourselves • Focus on the destination, not the journey

Code Component	Real World Manifestations (Negative)
	• Dependency on others • Susceptibility to being bought
Sex	• Shame mindset • Soulless; plesure-focused • Addiction • Performance anxiety • Aversion • Overexpectations • Manipulative tool • Force • Lack of communication
Anger	• Verbal or physical aggression • Indirect hostility: sarcasm, silence • Sabotage, revenge • Chronic irritability • Blaming mentality • Victim mentality • Repressed anger • Self-destructive behaviour • Intolerance
Disease	• Constant worry and stress about health • Social isolation • Pusing yourself too hard: excessive exercise or extreme diets

Code Component	Real World Manifestations (Negative)
	• Frequent medical visits or over testing • Destiny mindset • Procrastination in seeking medical aid • Low threshold for suffering • 'Why me' mindset
Religion	• Extremism • Intolerance • Feelings of guilt or shame • Extreme conformity • Extreme conservatism • Judgemental of non-aligned views
Complexes	• Feelings of unworthiness • Low self-esteem • Self-doubt • Social withdrawal or avoidance • Criticism of self and others • Unhealthy dependencies on others • Anxiety • Depression • Introversion • Self-destructive behaviours • Negative self-talk • Negative body image • Neglect or overcompensation in personal grooming

Code Component	Real World Manifestations (Negative)
	• Trust issues • Excessive need for control • Manipulation or dishonesty • Lack of open communication • People-pleasing for approval • Overreaction • Mood swings • Egocentric behaviour • Need for validation • Comparative or competitive behaviour • Impulsiveness • Indecisiveness
Loss	• Disorientatin and confusion • Anger • Denial • Numbness • Guilt • Inexpressiveness • Social withdrawal • Fatigue • Sleep issues • Appetite changes • Self-destructive behaviour • Self-doubt • Procrastination • Avoidance

Code Component	Real World Manifestations (Negative)
Failure	• Heightened levels of stress and anxiety • Lack of initiative and participation • Overthinking • Need for constant validation
Education	• Non-alignment with true calling • Non-alignment of passion with career goals • Destorted self-identity defined by by grades, brand of schools and colleges, or number of degrees • Comparative mindset • Feelings of inadequacy • Chronic performance anxiety • Self-worth defined by achievements

Step 4: Soul Mind Kriya Meditation Framework to Unearth and Erase the Programming

For all future references, the component and related manifestations will be called a 'file'. For example, a file of fear would contain all manifestations concerning the component of fear that matter to you. This means that we need to recall all memories of incidents or situations that led to our programmed responses. While observing this file in its entirety, try to unearth the defining situations that led to our set response pattern. The idea is to understand the reasons behind our programmed response. Upon deep introspection, we will be able to unearth these reasons.

Once we are able to clearly witness the foundational experiences of our early years, we will be able to reprogramme these deep-rooted circuits to align with our quintessential nature, our love hub.

The ideal manner to use this framework on an everyday basis depends on what you feel like addressing that particular day. Depending on your inclination, you will extract the corresponding file for deep introspection. The file will help you examine the manifestations and the code using memories to peel the layers of that code component. In this unearthing, the truth of the code will ultimately be revealed, exposing the extent of the corrosion of your source code.

The Soul Mind Kriya Meditation Framework

Below is a framework that most credible meditation techniques are based on, which can serve as a step-by-step guide to building our Soul Mind kriya.

1. Close your eyes and become aware of your breath.
2. Slow down your breathing. Slow and deep breathing reduces the hyperactivity of the monkey mind.
3. Clear your mind of any analysis, science, or logic.
4. Find a singular point of focus. Focus the mind on something fixed or even moving. This focal point can be outside or within the body.
5. Choose a 'file' that you want to unearth today. Remember, all manifestations of this component will form part of this file.
6. Create a witnessing energy to start going deeper.
7. Use memories to recall the images, emotions, and perceptions related to the file at hand. These references might begin with more recent memories and lead back to older ones. Note that most of your memories will come from the Beta and Alpha phases initially, which will lead you towards the defining scenarios of the Delta and Theta phases. The Delta and Theta phases are states of hypnosis where unconscious programming of the subconscious occurs. The primary code was written during these initial phases and reinforced by experiences in later years.
8. Delve deeper to unearth the reasons or incidents that created the code. Search your memory to reveal those defining scenarios. This involves deep questioning to peel the layers and uncover the truth. This truth may be pleasant or unpleasant; witness it with honesty. Come to terms with the reasons, circumstances, and people involved in the code's creation. This process will also clarify the root cause of all manifestations in this file.

For instance, one of the deep dives could reveal the following circuitry:

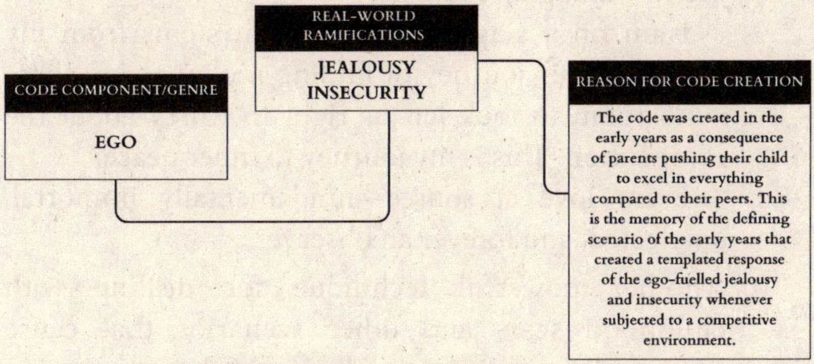

9. Now that you have unearthed the reasons for the code's creation, it is time to erase the subconscious programming associated with the file. Create thought energy inspired by love to help erase the materially inspired inner conditioning. We need to shift our attention to meditate on the undoing and fundamental correction of the concerned code. The first thought will recondition your mind to undo the corrupted code. You need to contemplate the source of the problem deeply and, more importantly, find a mind conditioner that will hit the sweet spot to undo the conditioning. Like a sculptor chiselling a block of stone until he creates the desired expression, you must drill deeper to uncover the thought energy that will undo the code. The more specific you are with your thought energy, the closer you will come to undoing the code. The principal aim of this first step is to use the love and unaffectable nature of our Soul Mind to erase the code. The second thought energy will also stem from your eternal home, the Soul Mind state of being. This

will be the phase of rewiring your code circuitry back to pure love. Continuing from the previous example, the two thoughts could be:

I am on a singular journey that stems from my truth. On this journey of finding my inner joy, there is no room to look left or right to worry about the competition. This is my journey to inner peace.

I am love at source—fundamentally immortal, unaffected, and forever an observer.

10. Another powerful technique for dealing with childhood scars and other scenarios that cause trauma, distress, or materially inspired programming is the 'inner counselling technique'. We need to go inwards and speak to the child within from a Soul-Mind perspective. The Soul Mind will counsel the child at the same point when the incident occurred, enlightening the young child's mind with the wisdom of the Soul Mind. This conversation can help undo the baggage the child (you) had to carry. This enlightened counselling by your Soul Mind can heal and erase any scar that left a lasting dent in the subconscious programming.
11. If contemplation is honest, you will witness the source light seeping in from the part you have started to erase. This is where the magic happens. You need to dissolve your consciousness into that source light as the only point of focus.
12. Create an intention to see more of the source light.
13. As you merge your Soul Mind with the source, you experience the bliss of nothingness yet everythingness—unbound awareness. You witness source energy

returning to your real soul self, and you may also receive signals, guiding you along the way to search for more of the source light.

14. Stay in this phase of nothingness, no mind, or pure love for as long as possible.
15. Rub your palms all over your body, imagining the source light emanating from your hands and spreading all over your body.
16. Finally, gently open your eyes.
17. Do not rush back to worldly awareness. Let the high of the deep meditation last for as long as it does.
18. Remember to reinforce the code-erasing thought and the thought inspired by the love hub as often as possible during waking moments. These codes tend to be stubborn and difficult to erase, requiring constant thought reinforcement over extended periods to finally get closer to the real you.

If you were to look at this kriya as a deep inner journey of self-discovery, you could get addicted to the practice itself. Every day when you extract a certain file, the discoveries of our subconscious coding and interconnected actions can empower you to step into the light of awareness.

To progress on this journey to uncover the real you and witness the state of bliss in your conscious moments, you must apply consistent efforts and have absolute faith in the process. As you progress in the experience of wiping the dust, the reasons to have kept the faith will become clearer.

The Soul Mind kriya has been designed to help you achieve a state of Soul Mind, which is the quest of all credible meditation techniques, leading you closer to your eternal home.

7

Exploring Identity, Purpose, and God

'The ego is only an illusion, but a very influential one. Letting the ego-illusion become your identity can prevent you from knowing your true self.'

—Wayne Dyer

Most of us ponder upon life's most fundamental questions during moments of solitude. These questions often revolve around the truth of our existence and the purpose of our presence on Earth. Throughout our lives, we define ourselves through our names and titles, but as we grow wiser, we seek deeper meaning.

Now that we have gone through our whole existence—from birth to death to the next birth—using the Soul Mind discovery, we should have better clarity on life's elemental question 'Who am I?' The answer is: I am not the positions, possessions, or titles. I am the eternal soul. The soul is the truth of existence for all humans and other forms of nature.

As we delve deeper into understanding and accepting our true selves, we will lift the veil on the other fundamental question of life, 'What is my purpose?' The answer to this lies in aligning all our actions in life with the yearning of our true self, the Soul Mind.

Having gone through the most comprehensive toolkit that can help us get back to our source, our true purpose should naturally flow. This is a phase of effortless doing and creating. We wake up every morning feeling light and free and do what we feel like doing that day. We dislodge ourselves from any targets to achieve or any goalposts to scale. There is clarity about our vision, without attachment to results. There is only the awareness of the present moment and what we intuitively feel like doing in that moment.

This is a baggage-free world with no pressures of the past or future. Everything feels light and easy. We fully immerse ourselves in the moment and relish it to the fullest. This can be called the state of unhindered flow.

Flow = transitioning from effort and results to effortlessness and bliss

We need to stay focused on embracing the elements of the self-love toolkit to achieve a state of flow. In our perseverance, we move from making intentional efforts to flowing effortlessly and intuitively from our love hub. When we eventually experience that deep inner alignment, we tune into our flow frequency naturally, and in this mind state, we script unbelievable feats aligned with us. Our very own Mona Lisa is created with intuitive awareness and a vision free of expectation.

When we commence our journey towards living intuitively, we experience the beauty of the journey itself. We naturally get drawn towards giving back to everything and everyone around us with a full heart. Nothing else is more satisfying than 'giving'. Many people find so much joy in this journey that they desire it over conventional experiences. Those who embark on this path and thrive are fortunate. According to the law of the spirit world, we are from nature and have a karmic responsibility to give back to it. The beauty of this life path is that the more you give, the more you receive.

The other big question we constantly seek answers to is: Is there a God? Religion often compels us to ponder upon related questions, such as: Is God watching over me? What deeds might lead to hell or heaven? Despite all our supposed belief in God, the moment something goes wrong, we tend to question our faith. Ironically, we remember God only when something goes wrong, and we lose faith in similar situations. For most of us, faith is this belief in God that has been drilled into our heads since our formative years. We grow up praying to idols in temples and churches, making these places of worship our destinations to meet and talk to God about our innermost secrets and concerns. This is the gospel truth for most of us.

Faith, in the context of *Sanyaas in the City*, is the belief in our innate connection with unity consciousness. Here, as we journey through life, we will come across moments where we will be tempted to lose faith in our guiding force, especially when something goes wrong. When we have a strong connection with our guiding force, it is important to understand that our Body Mind can and will be subjected to the good, the bad, and the ugly. The unsavoury circumstances in our lives are meant to be real-life teachings for us to make progress. It is a part of the awakening process. We need to be in a state of acceptance come what may. We must also possess 100 per cent faith in the synchronistic design of the occurrences to help us navigate the rough patches as much as we trust the source in our good times.

From this moment on, let us choose to live a life of unwavering faith because living in faith means living in freedom.

Afterword
Wisdom of the World

'Knowing yourself is the beginning of all wisdom.'
—Aristotle

The gamut of knowledge and information that hits us from all directions defines the course of our journeys. We are all exposed to stories from the East and the West where we hear about leading spiritual masters and their wisdom on the one hand and success stories of people on the material path on the other. The choices we make determine the nature of our experience of living.

We have noticed a growing interest in embracing Eastern wisdom, such as yoga and spirituality, in the West. Simultaneously, we have witnessed a surge of Western material influences on the East. This dynamic resembles a wheel of shifting influences across geographies and cultures.

This interplay between material and spiritual influences varies depending on our location, circumstances, and current yearning to uncover life's truths. At the peak of burnout in the West, the hippie movement emerged, emphasising a return to our true nature. While the goal was clear, the route often involved drugs interwoven with Eastern spiritual teachings to experience higher states of consciousness. This initial movement led to the unprecedented adoption of yoga and spirituality in the Western world. The profound influence of yoga is evident in the large numbers of Hollywood films that incorporate elements from this science. It is a mass movement that has created a strong connection between India and the USA, making them strategic, naturally aligned partners in contemporary times. Around the same time as the hippie movement in the West, the East was predominantly pivoted around the principles of yoga and spirituality.

Over time, this way of life in the Eastern world has progressively diluted due to the growing hunger for material gains. Life in the East during the 70s was characterised by peace, simplicity, and love. Fast forward to the present, and materialism has become dominant.

Ultimately, there is only one way to live a virtuous and fulfilling life—a life lived in free space and inspired by our truth. Embarking on the path towards liberation from material pursuits is an individual and unique journey. There is no definitive right or wrong position on this path. The pursuit of freedom is a deeply personal choice. Whether one is at the initial stages of contemplation, navigating the challenges of detachment, or fully immersed in the pursuit of spiritual enlightenment, the key lies in accepting and embracing and accepting one's current state and enjoying the process.

The emphasis is on being realistic and authentic with oneself, acknowledging that growth on this journey will unfold at its own pace. It is a continuous process of evolution as long as there is intent and effort. Moving on this path shouldn't be exhausting. It shouldn't turn you into a serious being but instead make you a more joyful person, living each day with enthusiasm and passion.

The real learning here is that, despite our different origins, the truth of human nature remains the same. We are nature and need to internalise this reality.

Our vision is for more people, across the world, to connect with our way of returning to nature. We aim to make your whole being joyful and loving. We want to make this world a beautiful place to live in. Our vision is to transform the lives of individuals worldwide, collectively harnessing the power of self-love to walk the path of *Sat chit ananda*—truth, consciousness, and eternal bliss.

being but instead makes you a more peaceful person. It integrates the [illegible] and passion.

The [illegible] is [illegible] core [illegible] the truth of human nature [illegible] the same. We are nature and need to internalise this result.

Our [illegible] with our way of returning to nature, [illegible] to make [illegible] world [illegible] warm and loving. [illegible] peaceful place to live in. [illegible] the lives of [illegible] collectively [illegible] the power of [illegible] truth, consciousness, and eternal bliss.

Index

The landscape of the material world we live in takes us from living in freeness to living in a cage.

Here's what is brewing in major metropolises worldwide.

The Fallout

Stress

Anxiety

Emptiness Despite

Achievement

Lifeless Journeys

Gripped Fearful Living

Blind Religious Leaning

Distressed Lifestyles

Health Complications

Meaningless Relationships

Overanalyses

Disconnection from Our Intrinsic Nature

Outward World Focus

Overdependence on Addictive Indulgences

Pushing People to Look for Solutions to Improve Their Life

Sanyaas, or the monk mind state, in the context of our chaotic urban setting

Sanyaas

Self-Love

Complete Inner Alignment

Freedom to Do and Be

Fearlessness

Intuitive Living

Witnessing Awareness

Understanding Consciousness

Mindfulness in Every Moment and Activity

Despite the City

Time Constraints

Occupational Demands

Meaningless Relationship Demands

The Need to be Seen Networking and Climbing

Living in a Concrete Jungle

Manic Schedules

Freedom and Fulfilment in Mindful Pursuits

Don't Wait for an Accident,

Take Charge TODAY!

The Naked Truth
Love More In = Love More Out

Time to truthfully acknowledge your departure from your real nature and the extent of depletion of your love hub.

Our love hub is at the heart of all our outward manifestations.

Understand the extent of this departure to also comprehend the need to fill it back up.

Barriers to Freedom and Self-Love

The barriers are a direct manifestation of our depleted love centre. The degree of depletion determines the intensity with which these barriers influence our lives.

FEAR: The Biggest Inhibitor
Overdependence of the Outer World
Unhealthy Physical and Mental Body
Ignorance of the Spirit World

The Secret Sauce

The Self-Love Toolkit

- Physical Body
  - Movement
  - Breath
  - Nutrition
  - Feel Good, Look Even Better
  - Sleep: Rest and Recovery
  - Sex
- Mental Body
  - Mind Control
  - Mind Clarity
  - Emotion Management
  - Mind Matters in Relationships
- Spiritual Body
  - Understanding Your Nature
  - Understanding Consciousness
  - Soul Mind Kriya

The Self-Love Toolkit

Physical Body

Movement

Shift the mindset to aspire towards your natural form. Kick-start your movement journey with the natural form flow.

Breath

Optimise the prana in the body and increase awareness with Pranayama and round-the-clock breath consciousness.

Nutrition

Intuitive eating, base theory, and a positive thought environment while eating and drinking can boost your understanding of the nutritional ecosystem.

Feel Good, Look Even Better

Personal grooming is an important aspect of self-care. When you look good, you feel better and vice versa.

Sleep: Rest and Recovery

Both qualitative and quantitative markers of sleep need to be assessed to optimise rest and recovery.

Sex

Be in the act with your Soul Mind—with all your bodily senses immersed—this will take you on a meditative journey that is an O to the power of many.

The Self-Love Toolkit

Mental Body

Mind Control

Make a subtle shift in thinking from your Body Mind to the Soul Mind to experience the real virtues of being the driver of your wheel.

Mind Clarity

The Soul Mind operates in a field of pure potentiality and absolute clarity. Start to see visibility around the fog that surrounds you in various situations.

Emotion Management

Clarity on the importance of staying full in your love hub will help you transcend from negative take emotions towards a more positive emotional ecosystem.

Mind Matters in Relationships

As you ascend from material to freedom, from Body Mind to Soul Mind, you witness an evolution in your relationships as well. You move from transactional take relationships to nurturing, joyful, and selfless give relationships.

The Self-Love Toolkit
Spiritual Body

Understanding Your Nature

We are nature ourselves, deeply interconnected with the nature around us. Having strayed away from our intrinsic truth, it is important to assess the extent of our disconnection from ourselves. This will open a world of truthful leanings towards everything in life and beyond.

Understanding Consciousness

Once you gain a sound understanding of the states of consciousness, it opens your mind to achieve the higher and more blissful states of transcendental consciousness.

Soul Mind Kriya

This revolutionary, easy-to-comprehend meditational technique will help you transcend your consciousness from the level of your body to your Soul, which is the fundamental quest of your journey to freedom.
You will be able to witness the meta-transformational effect of the dust being cleaned off your mind, leaving you feeling light and airy . . .

Adoption of the self-love toolkit will take us in the direction of thinking from the mind of our Soul Mind over our Body Mind.

Essence of the Soul Mind Thinking

We are not the body, we are the soul

and

The soul is immortal, unaffectable, incorruptible

↓

Love

Freedom

Purposeful living

Witnessing awareness

Zero thought state—in a field of infinite possibilities

Unwavering faith in the higher consciousness

↓

Sat Chit Ananda

Acknowledgements

I would like to express my heartfelt gratitude to my spiritual master, Yogiraj Gurunath Siddhanath, who initiated me into the life-transforming science of Kriya Yoga. Under his tutelage, my questions about the truth of life and beyond began to be answered, and my future direction became clear.

From my early years, I have been fascinated by the mystery of life, nature, and the worlds beyond. This curiosity led me to explore these subjects to satiate my natural yearning. I acknowledge that I have been deeply influenced by the writings of my guru, Gurunath Siddhanath, Osho, Dr Deepak Chopra, and luminaries from the world of science like Dr Bruce Lipton and Dr Amit Goswami.

One morning, when I was heavily into reading Osho's writings, I had a lucid dream where Osho spoke to me about taking Sanyaas to the city. This was the beginning of my quest to manifest this dream into reality.

Despite possessing no skill or background to write a book, I knew I had to make it happen. It was during this phase that I got in touch with Neha Sareen, a highly accomplished media personality, who was an erstwhile business partner and a nicely aligned spiritual mind to become a part of this incredible movement. Soon, the team came together, with

Neha, the iconic Dr Mickey Mehta—India's most recognised Wellness Guru, and Shikha Mehra—a corporate wiz turned wellness enthusiast with rich credentials in yoga and nutrition fully subscribing to the idea and working tirelessly to bring this book to life. I am deeply grateful for their shared vision and dedication.

I also extend my thanks to Ms Pallavi Puri, who joined Tata Sky as Chief Commercial Officer just as I was starting my entrepreneurial journey. Her critical presence in the media ecosystem made it possible for me to follow my passion and take wellness to the world.

One of the most important people in my life is my son, Aryaman. If God has special agents in this world, he would be one of them. A big shout-out to him for having helped us get off the ground with this book.

A heartfelt thanks to my dearest wife, Radhika who has been a rock in my life, always encouraging me in my pursuits. Much of what I know today comes from the life lessons of living with this beautiful soul.

Lastly, but most importantly, I am grateful to my parents, Air Marshal Shanti Gupta and Kusum Gupta, who created an environment for me to follow my inner truth rather than the herd. It was in this independent and free space that the miracles of my life unfolded with absolute synchronicity.

Looking back at the fifty-odd years of my life, I am convinced I am God's child. I know I am special and have His hand over my head to be and do good.

—Adarsh Gupta

I am deeply grateful to my mum, Poonam Sareen, for her unwavering strength, support, and love. Words cannot adequately describe the role she has played in shaping and influencing my journey, both in creating this book and beyond. Through all the milestones and crossroads in life, she has been my lighthouse, illuminating the path to a deeper spiritual immersion.

The hours and days we spent over many years decoding our experiential learnings, the big questions of life, the Bhagavad Gita, and the science of yoga awakened the seeker in me to my true calling. Just as my mum lovingly nudged me to step into my light, I knew I had to play a similar role in the lives of others—be their lighthouse. Very few people are blessed to have such an example in their own homes, and I will forever be grateful for that privilege.

During this process of awakening, I met my earth angel, Payal Mukherjee, who championed the writer in me to express herself. Though she is no longer with us on this physical plane, I will always be grateful to her for introducing me to Adarsh Gupta, who had a dream called 'Sanyaas in the City'. Today, that dream is on its way to becoming a reality. I vividly remember meeting him in a quaint coffee shop in New Delhi where he shared his vision with me. The purity of his intentions and the value he aimed to create in people's lives resonated deeply with me. Fellow dreamers and believers, Shikha Mehra and Dr Mickey Mehta joined the team, and I extend my heartfelt thanks to my co-creators for being voyagers with me on this enriching journey.

We dissolved our individual identities with the singular intention of creating a movement far bigger than what we independently stand for. That's how we did it. We've come a long way since that conversation in the coffee shop, and we still have much to do. This book is just the beginning.

We have also been blessed to have found a publisher like Hay House who lovingly worked alongside us to bring this dream to life. We would like to thank the entire team working behind the scenes, especially our editor, Sonali Pawar, for her dedication and support.

A special shout-out to my sister, Nisha Sareen Shewakramani, for always having my back. You show me how the strength of love can make you dance through life. My in-laws, Dr Beena and Anil Uppal, have showered me with their blessings, love, and support on this journey. Finally, to my husband, Vishal Uppal, who has patiently lent me his ear as I've brainstormed and shared our writings with him at different stages of development. He reminds me every day by example that living in love and from the soul can become our reality. Thank you, my love, for your quiet strength, encouragement, and belief in my potential.

—Neha Sareen

I want to start by thanking the most important person in my life, my mother, Poonam Mehra, my constant source of strength. I'm grateful for her unwavering love, support, and faith in me. If it weren't for her, I would not have had the courage to leave the corporate and step into the realm of wellness and this project would not have been an option.

As a child, I always used to wonder what kept my mother going and where she drew her strength from despite the challenges life threw at her. It was only later that I realised it was her years of sadhana under her guru and her belief in the

Supreme. I am deeply grateful for her absolute faith and life teachings, which shaped my own during my early years and laid the foundation for my spiritual journey.

I bow down to the Supreme for always looking after me and guiding me. It is only through his divine magical intervention that I crossed paths with Adarsh Gupta, whose vision, determination, and perseverance have brought this book to life. I am truly indebted to him for including me in his vision of bringing Sanyaas to the modern city world and bringing us together to lead this sacred mission. I'd also like to thank my co-authors Neha Sareen and Dr Mickey Mehta for being such warm and wonderful teammates. The last three years have been incredibly joyful and rewarding working alongside you.

The kind of person I've grown up to be in the last few years is because of the experiences and learnings I have had alongside my partner, my husband, Abhinandan. Thank you for always standing by my side, for pushing me out of my comfort zone, and for cheering me on. Your love, encouragement, and patience have been my anchor over the last three years, and I am grateful for your presence in my life. Lastly, I wouldn't have been able to fully commit to the project without the love and backing of my in-laws, Dr G. P. Rao and Ratna Gopalsetty, and my brother, Kshitij Mehra. Your blessings and encouragement have been a pillar of strength, and I am fortunate to have you all by my side.

—Shikha Mehra

Sanyaas in the City is a creation of divine predestined manifestation. It is the seamless coming together of the four of us—our leader, Adarsh, along with Neha, Shikha, and me—where our paths crossed, intercepted, and the minds got pollinated.

Looking at it with a child's heart and epistemological humility, the whole miraculously coming together of *Sanyaas in the City*, the labour of love of over three years has happened with the bewilderment and the innocence of childlike hearts of the four of us.

My early influences came from Maharishi Mahesh Yogi ji, Osho Rajneesh, and Deepak Chopra. They were the primary influencers and, in recent years, Baba Ramdev, Sadhguru, Ma Hansaji Yogendra, B. K. S. Iyengar, J. Krishnamurthy, Dr Bruce Lipton, and Dr Joe Dispenza. All of them I've read, many of them I've met or spoken to, and their lasting impressions find their way into my contributions to this book and beyond.

I would like to thank the invisible powers for helping me with my contribution to this book in a way that will hopefully plant a seed of realness and connectedness for our readers in the time to come.

—Dr Mickey Mehta

About the Authors

Adarsh Gupta is an alumnus of the Delhi School of Economics and has had an illustrious career in the FMCG and media industries, working on and with global brands such as Cadbury Schweppes, Nestle, Arnotts, Times Music and Entertainment, and HMV Saregama. In 2015, he ventured into entrepreneurship, driven by his passion for promoting fitness and wellness. His company, Brilliant Wellness, is the largest media firm in the wellness genre, offering 24x7 channels on Tata Play, Dish TV, and D2H. Adarsh is also the co-founder of Dominiche Productions, which has a scaled media play in the astrology and seniors' genres.

Neha Sareen is an alumna of the Mahindra United World College of India who has established herself as a versatile media personality over the last eighteen years. Following her passion, she has excelled as a prominent TV host, sports presenter, model, film journalist, and corporate emcee. Neha's professional journey took a transformative turn when she transitioned to content production. She embarked on creating compelling pop-spirituality shorts, including the digital series 'Transform with Neha', which deconstructs inspiring human stories. Neha has co-created and hosted the chat show 'Mind Positive with Neha Sareen', focused on fostering mental and emotional resilience.

Shikha Mehra is a graduate of St. Stephen's College, Delhi, and holds an MBA from the Indian School of Business (ISB), Hyderabad. After spending eight years in senior roles in the automobile and fintech sectors, she became a full-time yoga educator and nutrition consultant. Shikha has coached over 5,000 practitioners, helping them achieve healthier and fitter versions of themselves. She has been actively contributing to programming on the Tata Play Fitness channel. Shikha aims to inspire people to fall in love with themselves through the art of movement and mindful eating.

Dr Mickey Mehta is a leading holistic health guru in India, with 44 years of experience in holistic health and 53 years in the practice of yoga. He has been honoured as the 'Health and Wellness Icon of India' by the *Times of India* and has received the 'Pioneer in Holistic Health' and 'Award of Excellence' by the Ministry of Cultural Affairs in Switzerland during the 75th anniversary of Bharat ka Amrit Mahotsav. He is the author of four books, with four more in the pipeline. Dr Mehta has also written articles published in leading medical journals and has spoken at prestigious institutions such as Harvard University, IIMs, and IITs. Dr Mehta is associated with Jaslok Hospital, Asian Cancer Institute, ACI Cumballa Hill Hospital, Tata Memorial, Breach Candy Hospital, Ministry of External Affairs, Mumbai University, HSNC University, and Maharashtra State Police.

Notes and Reflections

Notes and Reflections

Notes and Reflections

Notes and Reflections